S0-BSO-837

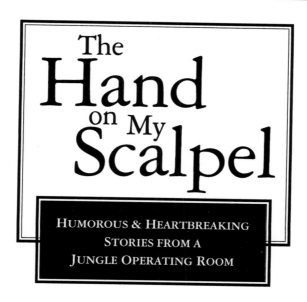

The Hand on My Scalpel

HUMOROUS & HEARTBREAKING STORIES FROM A JUNGLE OPERATING ROOM

DAVID C. THOMPSON, M.D.

CHRISTIAN PUBLICATIONS, INC.
CAMP HILL, PENNSYLVANIA

✛ CHRISTIAN PUBLICATIONS, INC.

3825 Hartzdale Drive, Camp Hill, PA 17011
www.christianpublications.com

Faithful, biblical publishing since 1883

The Hand on My Scalpel
ISBN: 0-87509-932-7
LOC Control Number: 01-131295

05   5 4 3

Chapters 1-4 are excerpted from *On Call*
by David C. Thompson.

*I dedicate this book
to the Teacher who came daily
to my operating room,
guided my hands,
cleared my mind
and reminded me often
that healing without Him
is impossible.*

Contents

FOREWORD

I f you want to understand medical missions, you have picked up the right book. And you won't be able to put it down after you have turned the first page. You will find an incredible panoramic picture that will pull you in—to the operating room table, by the bedside or preaching under a tree in the middle of Africa.

Dr. David Thompson will be your guide. You will go on rounds, work with limited resources, operate in the dark and bring people to Christ. You will fight mud, disease and ignorance. You will experience romance, financial difficulties, heartfelt gratitude and most of all, God's faithfulness. When your journey ends on the last page, you will realize what medical missions is all about because you will have experienced it. Which is, after all, the very best way to learn.

I heard of Dave long before I met him because he is a "giant"—one of a special class of doctors. There are only a few "giants" in a generation, and it is a privilege just to know them because they inspire, challenge and make you want to model your life and career after their example.

After serving as a missionary doctor in Kenya for eleven years, I love to challenge students and doctors to serve overseas. I was speaking at a missions conference of 350 medical students when I first saw Dave Thompson in a video. Another missionary speaker showed the video at the end of his presentation. Dave was passionately challenging an audience to respond to the Great Commission. His words moved me and many others at the conference. Before the day ended, seventy-five students made commitments to career missionary service.

When I finally met Dave Thompson recently, we felt an instant bond. I was impressed with his humble spirit and gentle manner. Knowing some of his "larger than life" story, I was reminded that God is not looking for superheroes. He simply wants people willing to follow Him. With that focus, God take average people—like Dave Thompson—and does extraordinary things for His kingdom.

Why is it so important to understand medical missions? Simply put, medical missions is one of the most effective methods for carrying the gospel around the world. Think about it. God could have sent His Son for a weekend to die on the cross for the sins of mankind. Instead, Jesus spent three years teaching, preaching and healing. His preaching proclaimed and moved people to belief and trust in God. His teaching taught us how to live in right relationships with God and man. His healing demonstrated His compassion and provided us an example to follow. Medical missions uniquely copies Christ's example. Doctors, nurses and other medical staff sacrificially serve to meet the overwhelming needs of suffering people.

In the U.S. there is one doctor for every 400 people. But where Dr. Thompson works, there may be one doctor for a community of 100,000 people. And that population—the size of a city—is riddled with parasites, plagued with malaria, malnourished and suffering from many other acute diseases that are easily treated.

Christ calls you and me to show them compassion so that they can see Him in us. When they do, the seeds of the good news fall on very fertile ground. People accept Christ by the thousands, churches are born and countries are transformed.

As you read on, you will soon realize that meeting overwhelming needs with limited resources is not easy. It takes a servant's heart, nights without sleep, resourcefulness and men and women who are faithful to God's call in the midst of great adversity. It takes Christians who are committed to "deny themselves, take up their cross and follow Him."

This book will fascinate you. It is a real life medical drama. But if that is all it is for you, it will be a tragedy. My hope is that David Thompson's words will move you to pray faithfully for the Thompsons and other medical missionaries around the world. Their success in ministry is proportional to how you and I pray. I also hope that their example will inspire you to a greater life of compassion and service on the mission field God has given you. God can work in you as He has worked in them to bring people to Himself. All you have to do is follow.

Who knows? God could even use this book to call you to overseas missionary service. Dr. Thompson and I would like that because the needs are great and the servants few. But more so, your commitment to missions will delight God. He has many people He wants *you* to introduce to His Son.

Dr. David Stevens, President
Christian Medical and Dental Society

INTRODUCTION

I am a general surgeon who with my wife and children has lived and worked in the central African country of Gabon as a medical missionary since 1977. During those years I have performed over 6,000 operations (not an unusually large number for a missionary surgeon). At least a third of the operations I performed were initially out of my area of expertise and training. Because most of the time there were no other surgeons to whom I could refer my patients, I learned to rely on God to help me as I operated (and learned). Again and again I sensed God guiding my hand and my scalpel.

Outside of the operating room He gave me wisdom and good judgment in caring for my patients. The net result was that, despite primitive conditions and limited medications, most of my patients recovered, some against astounding odds. But as you will see, this is not just a book about surgery. It's about God's ability to enable, guide, protect and teach His children in difficult circumstances. It's also about humor, since so much of what we do is really quite funny when viewed from God's perspective (and perhaps the reader's too).

I've always been slow to learn about the ways of God. For some reason it takes me two or three steps to discover something a wise person could figure out in just one.

Without the adventures and batterings in the joys and sorrows of everyday life, I would understand only superficially how serious God is about accomplishing His purposes on earth through people. Again and again I have seen God use ordinary people to do extraordinary things for His honor. Without these practical lessons, I would lack the conviction needed to conform my behavior to God's ways or speak about anything with passion.

All too often I have missed the point of the experiences God has taken me through and have wasted the pain or discomfort by blaming others or by giving in to frustration. In so doing, I have only made certain a later confrontation with the same problem. God keeps giving the same exam in different forms until I get the point. Mercifully, from time to time I have understood what He was trying to teach me after just one round.

These chapters from my boyhood as well as from my years as a surgeon in Africa recount some of those occasions. If they provide you a small step in understanding something about God's ways, power or wisdom, I will be delighted. If they simply help you to understand the process God uses to make us like Jesus, they will still have served a magnificent purpose.

David C. Thompson, M.D.
Bongolo, Gabon, West Africa
November 2000

Chapter
One

THE TELEPHONE CALL

The college cafeteria was still nearly empty at 7 a.m. on that wintry morning in February, 1968. I had just begun to eat breakfast when another student hurried into the cafeteria to tell me that there was an urgent, long-distance telephone call in the Dean's office, and that the Dean was holding the line open. I left my tray and hurried to his office, trying to imagine who might be calling me at this time of morning. A chill of premonition went through me as I climbed the steps and entered the building.

There were six or eight faculty and staff members in the room. The Dean greeted me solemnly and showed me to the phone. My heart was pounding. I wondered if the others could hear it. One of my teachers was gently trying to explain to me that something terrible had happened to my parents in Vietnam when the phone rang. The call was for me.

"Hello?"

"Hello, David? Is that you?"

"Yes."

"David, this is headquarters in New York. I don't know how to tell you this, but there has been heavy fighting in Vietnam over the Tet holidays. We have just received news that your mother and father have been killed by the commu-

nist forces." There was a pause. "David, we're all shocked and
so sorry."

As the Mission president paused, a hundred thousand images flashed through my mind, stopping finally at the last
day I saw my parents alive.

It was a warm, summer morning in Nyack, New York as
we stood outside our rented home and said good-bye. I had to
leave for work. Since Cambodia had closed to all missionaries,
my folks had agreed to go as missionaries to South Vietnam.
Their flight that day would take them to Saigon. There were
tears in our eyes as we hugged each other.

"Good-bye, Mom, Dad. I'll be praying for you that you'll be
safe."

"We'll be praying for you, David," Mom said. Dad was
strangely quiet for a moment, his eyes misted with tears.

"You may never see us again." His words seemed overly
dramatic. "No matter what happens, son, I want you to follow after Jesus."

I disliked mushy farewells and this was turning into one. I
smiled and hugged them again, my eyes dry, my heart unsus-
pecting.

"I'll be fine. You be careful!" I turned and walked away. At
the top of the bank I glanced back, waving to them once
more. They stood together, tears in their eyes, just looking at
me. Finally they waved back.

The rest of the telephone conversation, even the rest of
that day, remains shrouded in a kind of gray mist. I walked
alone across the campus to my room and locked the door. I
wept on my knees for what seemed like hours, but was probably less than forty-five minutes. All the while, a single word
filled my mind: *Why?* When there was no answer, a kind of

rage began to grow in my heart. *Why, God, why did You let this happen?* In reply—only the silence of an empty room.

Why don't You answer me, God? Don't You care about how I feel? Why won't You tell me why You let both my parents be killed now? If You made the worlds, why can't You give me an answer so I can understand why this happened? It was as though He did not want to answer. In the silence I struggled to understand a God who had saved my parents from death on previous occasions. What had they done wrong to deserve death this time?

I remembered how God had intervened when Mom and Dad had first gone to eastern Cambodia during the French-Indochina War. The roads were mined and cars were often ambushed by the nationalist rebels. The Mission had assigned them to Kratie, but there was no safe way to get there. The French military authorities discouraged them from even attempting to drive, but when they saw that my father was determined to go, they counseled him to wait for a military convoy. Dad felt this was just as dangerous as traveling alone and told the French commandant that he preferred to travel by himself. God had sent them to Cambodia and if God wanted them to preach the gospel in Kratie He would have to protect them on the way.

The French commander was appalled that Dad would even contemplate such a risk. Didn't the Reverend Thompson know that the rebels had skewered French children on upright poles as a warning to foreigners to get out of their country? Did the Reverend think that he looked any different than a Frenchman? But Dad was not to be deterred. Reluctantly, the commander agreed to let them travel alone. He advised Dad to drive as fast as the roads permitted and warned him not to stop under any circumstances—an invitation for ambush, he said.

I was too small to remember the trip but I heard the story many times from my mother. She told how Dad drove at breakneck speed and finally broke a spring on the rough road. While Mother desperately prayed for our safety, he stopped the jeep to survey the damage. A French army truck full of troops came up behind us. For a wonderful moment we thought that the Lord had sent the troops along to protect us, but to our dismay, the truck swept on by in a cloud of dust. One hundred yards down the road, the truck hit a land mine and overturned. While we watched in horror, rebels hiding in the bushes poured gunfire into the burning wreckage, killing everyone. Had God not stopped our car with a broken spring, we would have been the victims.

The second time God spared Dad and Mom was even more dramatic. Dad told the story publicly so many times that I know it by heart. We had been in Kratie for perhaps a year. French troops were garrisoned in the city because it was a provincial capital. One day the French commander received secret information that a large force of rebels was going to attack the French rubber plantations outside of the town of Snoul, eighty kilometers away. Confident that his information was correct, the commander loaded his troops on trucks and raced to Snoul, hoping to surprise the rebels. The purported attack never materialized. It was a rebel trick.

The actual plan was for a rebel force of about 2,000 to attack Kratie where we lived. As dusk fell, a soldier knocked on our door and asked if we would like to come to the hotel where the few remaining French soldiers were planning to fight to the finish. Father thanked him, but said no. Instead, he said, he and his wife would pray. God had not brought them to Kratie to be destroyed before they had done the work they were sent to do.

I remember having to stay under the bed with my sister while Dad and Mom knelt and prayed. Mom said we were very fussy and made it hard for them to pray. As Dad told it, around 2 a.m. a white flare lit up the square between our house and the hotel. The attack on the hotel started soon after.

Bullets flew everywhere. Suddenly, a red flare shot up and burned briefly in the night sky. The shooting tapered off. In the morning there was no sign of the rebels and nobody understood why the rebels had abandoned the attack. The French commander returned later that day from Snoul and was surprised to find the city intact.

In 1955 the French granted independence to Cambodia, returning power to the king of Cambodia. The king promised amnesty to all the rebels who would turn in their weapons and pledge allegiance to him—some of the rebels were communists. On the announced day, the provincial rebels came by the thousands to the town square and stacked their weapons in a great pile. There were speeches and ceremonies all day. Toward the middle of the day, the retiring French commander asked Dad to translate for him while he spoke to the rebel commander. After the introductions, the commander asked the rebel leader, "Why did you not take the city the night we were diverted to Snoul, leaving Kratie defenseless?"

The rebel commander seemed surprised by the question. He remembered the night very well, he said, and suggested that the French commander was mistaken, for when the rebels attacked Kratie they were confronted by thousands of French soldiers. There were troops everywhere—more than he had seen at any other time during the war! Since his rebel force numbered only 2,000 men, they had decided to flee.

With Dad interpreting, the French commander and the rebel leader argued about the events of that night. Only Dad understood what had happened: the army of the Lord had saved us. God's angels had appeared as French soldiers in such great numbers that the rebels withdrew.

As I wept alone in my college room, I heard God speak to me for the first time in my life. Although I did not hear a voice or audible words, I knew and understood what He was saying to me.

"David, do you trust Me?"

What does that have to do with anything? I wondered. Of course I trusted Him! Didn't He know that I had given my life to Him and followed His ways obediently from the time I was five years old? Even as a child, had I not trustingly invited Him to live in my heart? As I waited, He spoke again.

"David, do you trust Me?"

What was I supposed to answer? I had already dedicated myself to serve Him as a missionary doctor.

I remembered that day, too. I was fourteen years old, traveling in Cambodia with our family, riding in the back of the Land Rover. We had been driving for about six hours on a pot-holed road when we saw a smashed-up truck ahead. On the opposite side of the road was a bus with the front end damaged. People were scattered along both sides. We stopped the Land Rover and got out. A man informed us that the two vehicles had been approaching each other at high speed. Pointing to a large pot-hole in the center of the road, he explained that the truck had swerved to miss the pothole and had hit the oncoming bus head-on only minutes before our arrival.

Father knew a little about treating sores and injuries, so he asked if anyone was seriously injured. The man pointed to the bus driver propped up against a nearby mango tree. He was probably going to die, we were told. Father motioned for me to come with him.

A group of onlookers stood around the injured man, watching helplessly as he struggled to breathe. Periodically he coughed up blood. The group parted to let us get closer to him. After hesitating a moment, Father knelt down next to the bus driver and introduced himself in Cambodian. The man nodded in acknowledgment. It was obvious even to me that unless someone did something soon he would die. I knew that there was no hospital within 300 kilometers. While I poured the man a drink of water from our thermos, Father asked him if he felt ready to meet God. The man slowly shook his head. Would he like to know how he could get to heaven? Father persisted. The man looked at Dad for a long time, his chest heaving with every breath. Then he looked at me. Despair filled his eyes as he coughed up a large amount of blood.

"Please, don't talk to me now about your God!" he gasped. "Just help me not to die!" With great sadness Dad looked at him and shook his head.

"I don't know how to help you," he said. The man took several more swallows of water and turned his head away. Father motioned for me to come back to the car. We walked in silence, aware that the man would not last more than a few minutes and knowing that without Christ he would spend eternity in hell.

The rest of the trip I said very little, reliving the entire experience. Over and over I heard the man's desperate pleas and felt again our helplessness. If only we could have helped him to live, perhaps he would have listened to us and perhaps he would have received Christ. The more I thought about it, the more I knew what I wanted to do with my life. I wanted to help the sick people of the world who had no one to help them so that, unlike this man, they would live to hear about Christ's love and believe in

Him. By the time we reached Phnom Penh I had solemnly promised God that I would devote my life to that task.

It was some time until I was told how brutally my mother and father had died. I learned that they had been shaken from their sleep in the early morning hours when North Vietnamese infiltrators blew up Carolyn Griswold's house next door. In the dark, with firing all around, Mom and Dad had heard her cries but had been unable to rescue her. In the light of day, they discovered that her father too had been crushed in the wreckage.

Two days later, as the battle for the city of Banmethuot raged around them, Mom and Dad huddled in a neighboring missionary's house. North Vietnamese soldiers entered their house and blew it up. Realizing they were no longer safe in any of the houses, they all took refuge in a bunker hastily dug in what had been the trash pit.

When the North Vietnamese finally took the city of Banmethuot, they did not permit my parents nor the other missionaries with them to surrender. Instead, they cruelly mowed them down with machine gun fire. As Mom crouched and Dad stood in a bunker behind the mission house, his hands in the air, the North Vietnamese finished them off with hand grenades. Only one missionary, Mrs. Marie Ziemer, survived to tell the story.

My encounter with God after my parents' death only underscored my need to trust God with the people and things that were most precious to me. I had already learned through experience that God was trustworthy by the dramatic way in which He had provided for me to go to Geneva College.

Chapter
TWO

THE MIRACLE

A friend studying pre-med at Geneva College spoke so enthusiastically about the school that I decided to apply. I was accepted into the freshman class of 1966. Quite naive about college and thinking I would have to get top grades before I could even qualify for a scholarship, I did not apply for any student aid before arriving.

The Mission promised a monthly allowance which at that time amounted to a little over $100. All of my assets combined did not amount to even one-fourth of the expected annual expenses. Nevertheless, remembering Mother's statement that if God wanted me to become a missionary doctor He would provide the money, I believed that He would supply, although I didn't know how.

The seriousness of what I was expecting God to do did not really dawn on me until registration day. I found my way down to the school gymnasium where registration tables were set up. All went well until I arrived at the cashier. She took my registration card and after ringing up all the courses I was signed up for and adding my room and board, she announced that my bill for the first semester was several thousand dollars. I handed her $50 that my dad's brother had given me. The cashier was not impressed, particularly since I had no loans, grants or scholarships lined up to cover even half of the fees. She directed me to another table where a nice lady from the finance office asked me how I intended to pay my bill.

With some hesitation I explained that I was expecting God to provide the money. Her mouth did not drop open, but it might as well have. She got up, walked toward a serious-looking man in a dark suit and pointing back at me, handed him the bill. My six foot three inches felt like only three inches as he motioned for me to come over. He introduced himself as the Dean and asked what arrangements I had made to pay for my first semester. This time I remembered to mention that I was planning to work part-time. I told him that I was trusting God to provide the rest. He seemed sympathetic, but said that I would have to talk with him in his office later in the week and that perhaps I would have to take out some loans. My heart sank at those words. How could I pay back school loans on a missionary salary?

Classes started the next day, and that same day I began looking for work. I didn't know anyone in Beaver Falls, and I didn't even know where to look for work. Besides, I didn't have a car, so getting work in town was not a practical option. Having grown up in Asia, I knew how to work, but I didn't know how one went about finding a job. My first job in America had been helping a neighbor build a retaining wall behind his house. He outlined how he wanted the bank dug out and the dirt moved elsewhere and how he wanted railroad ties stacked to hold up the bank. I worked alone ten hours a day, digging dirt and hauling it away in a wheelbarrow. During the second week it began to drizzle. In Cambodia, men didn't stop working unless it rained heavily and this was only a typical North American all-day drizzle.

As the day wore on, the ground turned to mud and I became thoroughly drenched. Although the rain and mud made the work more difficult, I carried on and thought little of it. When my employer returned home and saw me, he was speechless. Did I not know not to come to work on a rainy day?

The second week at Geneva I learned that the college was looking for someone to clean the bathrooms in the men's dormitory. The pay was $1 an hour. I signed up immediately, wondering why no one else seemed interested. I soon learned that cleaning toilets was not a job to dawdle over. I became so expert that I usually got the job done in under an hour. That meant that I was earning less than a dollar a day. I soon realized that I would never pay my way through college cleaning toilets.

The second week of school, the director of the college's sixty-voice a capella touring choir announced tryouts. My roommate, David MacMillan, had a rich baritone voice, and he was accepted immediately. He urged me to join too. The idea appealed to me. I had enjoyed choir in both high school and church, and although my tenor voice was a bit reedy, I was better than average at reading music, and I could harmonize. I determined to try out the following Monday. Just to be sure that I would get in the choir, I began praying about it.

On Sunday I came down with a cold. By Monday morning I could hardly talk. I was irritated that the Lord had not kept me from getting a cold at such an important time in my life. Perhaps the Lord would make the choir director understand. Supremely confident that God was smoothing the way in response to my prayers, I tried out.

By the time I got to his room, the choirmaster was tired and grouchy. He asked me what part I sang, and when I croaked that I sang tenor, he handed me a hymnal opened to a song he had selected. I started to explain to him that I couldn't sing because I had laryngitis, but he glared at me over the top of the piano and ordered, "Sing!" When he'd heard about ten seconds worth, he stopped playing, thanked me, and, brushing aside my efforts to explain, called for the next student.

The following day my name did not appear on the list of those accepted. I was angry at the Lord. Hadn't I prayed about it? That was always supposed to work. Yet He had done nothing to help me. It seemed to me that God had botched the job, but since Christians aren't supposed to think that way, I tried to forget about the whole thing.

One day, I noticed that most of my dormmates were coming to class in wrinkled shirts. The Thompson Ironing Service was born. I had never ironed a shirt in my life, but I borrowed an iron and an ironing board and began ironing for 25 cents a shirt. It still wasn't enough.

My typing skills were better than average, and I had a good typewriter, so I offered my typing services at 15 cents a page. Corrections were an extra 10 cents a page. Soon I was busy every evening ironing shirts, typing papers and cleaning toilets. When those jobs were done, I got down to studying, often until 1 or 2 in the morning. The Dean hadn't contacted me yet, and I wondered how long it would be before he called me in for "the discussion." I wasn't about to remind him.

About four weeks into the term, the school administration announced that there would be a freshman talent show. My roommate and I decided to enter. For weeks we worked on a humorous musical skit I wrote in which we acted and sang. Dave had an evening job cleaning the classrooms in a nearby elementary school. As we mopped the floors together, we practiced. By the day of the show we had the skit down to perfection.

There were many good presentations, but our skit was one of the best. We won a prize. As we filed out of the gymnasium, the choir director approached me.

"David, that was a very good skit you two put on!" I looked up, surprised that he would remember my name. I smiled and thanked him.

"You know, you really can sing tenor after all!" Now he had my interest. "I need tenors in the choir and I'd like you to join. How about it?" I sadly explained to him that although I wanted very much to sing in the choir, because I had to work to earn money for school, I didn't have the time. He seemed genuinely disappointed, but not as much as I.

That afternoon I found a note in my mailbox from the Dean, asking me to come to his office the next morning. My heart sank.

I counted up all of my earnings. I had spent all of the allowance money from the Mission to buy books. I entered the finance office with a sense of impending doom. The Dean greeted me warmly and got right to the point.

"Well, David, has the Lord provided you with the funds for your first semester at school?"

"Not entirely, sir." I placed my $150 on the desk in front of me. He looked at it briefly, then at my bill.

"Have you considered a school loan?" he asked. I explained to him why I didn't want to take out any loans. He looked at me thoughtfully.

"Mr. Greig talked to me yesterday, and it seems he really wants you to sing in his choir."

"Yes, he did ask me to join the choir, but I had to refuse. Now that I'm working, I don't have time to sing in the choir three afternoons a week and study too." The Dean nodded and continued nodding, obviously thinking hard.

"Let me ask you this, David," he said finally, making his hands into a steeple. "If we were to find some grants and scholarships to pay for your first semester here in school, would you consider quitting the jobs you have to sing in the choir?" I stared at him, my mouth ajar.

"Do you mean not work and sing in the choir?" I finally asked.

"That's right. Your professors tell me you're an excellent student. If you keep your grades up, I think we might be able to find you other scholarships next semester." I wanted to kiss the man!

As I walked out the door, my feet barely touching the ground, I realized I had seriously misjudged the Lord. Actually I realized so many things at once that it took days for me to sort it all out. I remembered a promise that I had learned as a child: "Trust in the LORD with all your heart and lean not on your own understanding; in all your ways acknowledge him, and he will make your paths straight" (Proverbs 3:5-6).

That night I asked God to forgive me for failing to trust Him.

Chapter Three

MEDICAL SCHOOL

After the death of my parents, I decided that although I could no longer dream of working alongside them, I could follow in their footsteps. Life took on a new urgency and I decided to go to summer school in order to graduate from Geneva College in three years instead of four. God continued to provide for my financial needs through a combination of grants, scholarships, speaking honorariums and gifts, particularly from members of the Beaver Falls Alliance Church.

The challenge of getting into medical school seemed almost insurmountable. The collegiate and postgraduate landscape was littered with those who had tried and had been rejected. Then, of course, there was the ever-present problem of finances.

God had certainly provided for me in response to my mother's faith. Now she was gone. Would He do the same in response to my faith? Admittedly filled with doubt, I wrote to six medical schools, all in Pennsylvania. The school I wanted most to attend was the University of Pittsburgh School of Medicine. It was considered to be one of the most difficult to get into.

I began filling out applications. All had one question in common: "Why do you want to become a doctor?" They wanted an essay-type answer, preferably truthful.

I was greatly perplexed by the question. It was not that I didn't know the answer—I wasn't certain that the truth would be acceptable. If I wrote that I wanted to become a doctor because I felt God calling me to become a medical missionary, they would no doubt laugh hilariously and throw my application into the trash.

As I prayed about what to do, I remembered the story of Gideon putting out the fleece. I sensed the Lord's approval as a plan formed in my mind. I would divide the six applications into two piles of three. On one set I would write the truth, but only part of it. I would say that I wanted to become a doctor because I loved the idea of helping sick people get better. On the other three I would write the same thing but I would include my call from God. The question then became, in which pile would I put the application for the University of Pittsburgh?

After much soul-searching and prayer, I put it in the "whole truth" pile. I committed the matter to the Lord and mailed the applications. Now all I had to do was wait for a request for an interview from several or all of them.

I never heard from the three schools in the "part truth" pile; but two of the three schools that knew about my call to become a missionary doctor responded by asking for an interview. One was the University of Pittsburgh. I was to report to the Children's Hospital in Pittsburgh for an interview with Dr. W.B. Kiesewetter, the Chief of Pediatric Surgery.

On the appointed day, I drove to Pittsburgh from Beaver Falls. A sense of panic gripped me as the hour for the appointment approached. It was difficult finding a parking place. When I finally found Dr. Kiesewetter's office, his secretary asked me to be seated and took my file in to him. Ten minutes later Dr. Kiesewetter buzzed for me to come in.

Dr. Kiesewetter was a trim, distinguished-looking man, with white hair and reading glasses far down on his nose. He turned, looked over the rims, then stood and shook my hand. His smile was friendly but formal. He asked me to be seated.

"I've been looking over your application, David, and I found it to be somewhat . . . uh . . . unique." I felt my stomach contract. "Tell me, what do you mean by your statement that God has called you to be a doctor?"

I swallowed hard and told him about witnessing a man die when I was a fourteen-year-old in Cambodia and that I felt God had permitted me to see that to call me into missionary medicine.

"How do you know it was God?" he asked.

"Well, He spoke to me in my heart," I explained. It sounded weak, and his raised eyebrow confirmed it.

"How? Did you hear His voice?"

"Uh . . . no. He just spoke to me in my . . . uh . . . heart and I knew that He wanted me to do that." Although it was March and the room was cool, I felt sweat trickling down my ribs under my white shirt. He nodded skeptically and turned back to the application.

"If you become a doctor, then, you're going to preach to people?"

"Well, I want to share my faith in Jesus Christ with them if I can," I explained, trying to stifle feelings of despair at the way the interview was going. "But not if they don't want to hear about it."

"What do you believe about Jesus Christ?" Dr. Kiesewetter asked, leaning back in his chair. "I thought He was a good man who was misunderstood and crucified about 2,000 years ago."

"I believe He is the Son of God, that He came to earth to die for the sins of the world and that after He died on the cross, He rose again from the dead." It came out in a rush, like I was reciting something I'd memorized in Sunday school. Dr. Kiesewetter did not pursue it.

"I see that your parents are missionaries in Vietnam. Do you plan to join them?" He had stumbled onto the one subject I had hoped to avoid. I had no choice but to answer.

"Uh . . . my parents *were* missionaries in Vietnam, but they're not anymore," I explained weakly, hoping it would be enough. It wasn't.

"Where are they now?"

"They're in heaven."

Dr. Kieswetter looked up sharply, then softened. "I'm sorry. Did it have something to do with the war?"

"They were killed last year by North Vietnamese soldiers during the Tet Offensive." My answer visibly rocked him.

"I'm very sorry, David. I guess I did read about that in the paper. Do you mind talking about it?"

"I don't mind talking about it," I said, wondering how he'd react.

"How do you feel about it?" Hesitantly, reluctantly, trying not to sound psychopathic, I explained how I had learned to trust God, how I believed that God had a purpose in my parents' death that I did not understand, but that was ultimately good. Dr. Kiesewetter asked many more questions, finally asking me to explain why I believed in the Bible. His questions were not unfriendly, but they exposed me for what I was: a fundamental Christian who actually believed that the Bible was God's inerrant Word; that God still speaks to people and that people who reject Christ or who have never heard of Him will go to a real hell; that Christians have a responsibility to tell the world about Jesus Christ and that Jesus

Christ will some day return to earth in the clouds. Never once did he indicate approval or agreement.

The interview had lasted for nearly an hour, and all I wanted to do was escape. Dr. Kiesewetter removed his glasses and leaned back in his chair. A slight smile played at the corners of his mouth and he looked at me directly.

"I haven't been entirely honest with you," he said finally. Although slightly numb, I noticed that there was a different look in his eye. He continued, a smile spreading across his face. "I want you to know, David, that I too am a Christian." He chuckled at the look of surprise and relief on my face.

"David," he continued, "I want to commend you for your courage today. I only wish that when I was in your position many years ago, I had had the courage to speak about my faith in Jesus Christ as openly as you have."

I didn't know how to respond, so I just listened, gripping the arms of my chair.

"I want you in our medical school," he continued, "and I want you to know that I am prepared to do everything in my power to see that you are accepted." In a daze, I thanked him, shook his hand and stumbled back to my car. How had it happened, I wondered, that out of the hundreds of doctors on the faculty of the University of Pittsburgh, a Christian doctor had been chosen to interview me?

Several years later, Dr. Kiesewetter told me that the Dean of the medical school had called him up two weeks before the interview. The Dean knew that Dr. Kiesewetter was an outspoken Christian and very active in the Christian Medical Society.

"Bill," he had said, "I have an application here for our medical school. This guy's so hot I thought I'd better send him to you! You'll see when you get the application." The application was mine.

That year there were 2,200 applications for 100 positions in the first-year class at the School of Medicine. While it was true that most candidates applied to several schools, the Dean estimated that there were at least five qualified students for every position available in the United States. Two weeks after the interview, I received notification from the university that I had been accepted to the freshman class starting September, 1969. It was a dream come true—accepted at the medical school of my choice—but still no money!

About a week later, Dr. Kiesewetter called me on the telephone and invited me to have dinner with him and his wife the following Friday night. After dinner we would all go to a hockey game. I immediately accepted and wrote down the directions.

I was impressed by the large, three-story, beautifully preserved home. I rang the front doorbell. The doctor opened the door and welcomed me in. Never in my life had I been in a house with such plush carpet and lovely furnishings. Dr. Kiesewetter introduced me to his wife, and I immediately sensed that I had found a new friend. Since dinner was ready, she led us directly into the dining room.

The sight of the beautifully set table triggered a wave of inner panic. There were two forks, two knives, two goblets and two sets of plates at each place. How was one to know which to use first? Sitting down, I barely averted dipping the end of my tie in the soup!

Mrs. Kiesewetter turned and asked if I would like white wine with my meal. I felt my face turning pink. If I said yes, I would have to drink it, and I did not like alcohol. If I refused, they might think I was "holier-than-thou." Mrs. Kiesewetter sensed my predicament. "Are you accustomed to drinking wine with your meals? I know that not everyone is." I gratefully mumbled a negative reply.

By this time, Dr. Kiesewetter had selected a spoon for his soup. Now I knew which one to use. The dinner went smoothly, and I began to enjoy myself. After dinner, we headed downtown to watch the Pittsburgh Penguins. I had never seen ice hockey, and the Kiesewetters had season tickets for seats in the second row on center ice. Although it seemed to me that there was a great deal of violence, I was amazed at the skill of the players and the speed of the game.

After the game we returned to the Kiesewetter's home for ice cream and coffee. Dr. Kiesewetter turned to me.

"David, the reason I asked you to come this evening was so that Mrs. Kiesewetter could meet you." He paused and looked at his wife as if to confirm something. "Now that she's had a chance to get to know you, we would like to invite you to come live with us while you're attending medical school." For a moment I thought I'd misunderstood him, but as I played his words back in my mind, I realized what he had said. These people hardly knew me, yet they were offering to let me live in their home. For a moment I couldn't think of anything to say.

"I think that would be wonderful," I finally blurted. "I'm so surprised I don't know what to say!"

"Of course, we would want you to eat with us when we're home," Mrs. Kiesewetter explained, "and we would expect you to help in the yard and around the house."

"Your staying in the house will help us, too," Dr. Kiesewetter added, as if I needed convincing. "We are often away on trips, and this way the house won't be empty." I tried to imagine what it would be like to live in such a beautiful house.

"I'd be happy to take care of the yard work and anything else you might want me to do," I assured them.

And so, in the space of a few hours, the problem of food and lodging was settled. I sang praises to God at the top of my lungs as I headed my Volkswagen Bug back to Beaver Falls.

It gradually began to dawn on me that the Lord intended to provide for all of my needs, including the thousands of dollars I would need each semester for tuition and books.

Two weeks after that memorable evening, Dr. Kiesewetter phoned again. He knew of a group in Philadelphia called the Pennsylvania Medical Missionary Society. This organization provided conditional grants to medical students planning to become missionaries. If the student served overseas for at least ten years, the grant became a gift. Dr. Kiesewetter explained that he had called their president and asked her to send me an application. I sent the completed application to Dr. Kiesewetter who added a strong letter of recommendation and forwarded it to the society.

One month later, as I read their letter of response, my hands began to tremble: the Pennsylvania Medical Missionary Society was agreeing to pay for my tuition and my books! During the four years that followed, God so wonderfully provided through them and others that in 1973 I graduated from medical school essentially debt-free.

On graduation day, as I walked up the steps and was handed my diploma, I wished that my parents could be there to rejoice with me. But even as I wished, I knew that they had already given me everything I needed to follow in their footsteps, especially their example of faith in God.

Chapter

Four

THE MITCHELLS

I have a picture to prove that when I was fourteen months old I was present at the Mitchell's oldest daughter's first birthday. Of course, I don't remember anything about that encounter, but I do remember meeting Archie and Betty Mitchell in 1954 when I arrived at the Dalat School for Missionary Children in Dalat, Vietnam at the tender age of six.

Mrs. Mitchell was my dorm mother. She was firm and fair and at first a little awesome. She seemed to know a great deal about what went on in the hearts and minds of little boys. She was also a great story reader to lonely little boys, and she gave a great scrub, even if you were the fifteenth dirty little kid in the bathtub lineup. Mr. Mitchell, our dorm father, was even more awesome than Mrs. Mitchell because he was very tall and had a scar on his chin.

In later years, I learned that he was the only survivor of an explosion from an incendiary balloon bomb that the Japanese had floated over to the United States during World War II to set the forests on fire. At that time, Mr. Mitchell was a young pastor in Bly, Oregon.

One day, he and his wife took a group of children on a Sunday school picnic in the woods. While he was unloading food from the car the children discovered the unexploded bomb. Archie shouted a warning, but it was too late. A tree protected Archie from the blast and he survived, but his wife and all the children were killed in the explosion. They were the only civilians who died on the U.S. mainland during World War II as the result of hostile enemy action.

Mr. Mitchell had big, hard hands that were very gentle in the bathtub but unforgettable when applied to one's bottom. From the time I came to school until I was ten years old, I lived with the Mitchells in the dorm eight months out of every year. They provided a stability to dorm life that I liked. Living with them was very much like living with a favorite aunt and uncle.

I have already mentioned the Mitchell's oldest daughter, Rebecca. She was a tomboy. To the shame of all the boys, she could run faster and farther, jump and climb higher and play softball, basketball and just about every other game as well or better than any of us. She seemed to delight in proving that in every area she was better than the boys.

The fact that her parents were the Mitchells made the situation particularly difficult. She made a great point of telling us that if we touched her, her father would squish any one of us "like a bug." It seemed totally plausible, and naturally this did not endear her to us.

The Mitchells had three other children, all of whom I thought were nicer than Becki.

When I was eleven, the Mitchells returned to the United States. After one year of furlough, they tried to go back to South Vietnam, but the government refused to grant them visas until the following year. When they finally were able to return, the Mission assigned them to work in the city of Banmethuot in the central highlands.

Becki enrolled in school as an ordinary missionary kid like the rest of us. She was still very athletic and as competitive as ever, but she no longer tormented us. In ninth grade, I finally grew past her, and as I matured physically and athletically, she no longer posed a threat to my self-esteem. I liked girls to pay attention to me and did my best to impress them. Becki would not be impressed, and so I ignored her—until one day when her father was kidnapped by the Vietcong.

Mr. Mitchell was the director of the Leprosy Hospital about fifteen miles outside of Banmethuot. The staff included one missionary doctor, Dr. Ardel Vietti, and a number of other workers, including Dan Gerber, a young Mennonite agriculturalist. The Mitchell children had just arrived home for vacation when the first warnings of trouble came: three bridges leading to the leprosarium were burned by the Vietcong. They also posted a warning against repairing the bridges. The missionaries, certain that the Vietcong were not interested in them personally, continued their work at the leprosarium, fording the streams when they had to drive into Banmethuot.

On the evening of May 31, 1962 the Vietcong struck again. As Mrs. Mitchell and the children watched in horror, the Vietcong tied Mr. Mitchell's hands behind his back and marched him into the jungle, along with Dr. Vietti and Dan Gerber. No one ever saw or heard from any of them again.

The news of Mr. Mitchell's kidnapping shocked all of us. After all, if it could happen to Mr. Mitchell, it could happen to anyone's parents.

When the missionary kids returned to school a month later, we watched the Mitchell children with a sense of awe. They did not talk very much about their father. We never saw them crying, although I'm sure they did. Their lives went on as before, except that now they shared a common sorrow that bound them tightly together. I remember wondering how they could stand it day after day not knowing where their father might be or what he might be suffering. But I dared not ask. *What if it had been my father? Would he be locked up in a bamboo cage? Would he be tortured? Marched every day through the jungle? Chained in an underground Vietcong cave?* The thought of it left me shaken and fearful. *How could they stand it?* It was a great mystery, one that I did not understand until many years later.

In 1965, I left Dalat School for the last time. I don't remember saying good-bye to the Mitchells. It seemed to me that in an indefinable way their experience had left them a cut above the rest of us. After the death of my own parents six years later in that same city of Banmethuot, I learned that in the school of life, there is no better teacher than godly sorrow.

During my years at Geneva College I kept a sharp eye out for the right girl. I was certain that I would find her during college, since bachelorhood did not appeal to me. Finding the right girl, however, turned out to be more of a challenge than I had imagined. To begin with, I was still trying to figure out the American system of courtship. I was often perplexed. The social structure at Dalat School was designed to discourage kids who lived together from sunup to sundown from getting into serious romances. With such clearly defined goals, circumvention was a relatively simple matter. But my being an artist in manipulating the Dalat social system did not help at all in the United States.

During my senior high school year in America, after several humiliating efforts at dating, I decided not to try anymore. But teenage hormones being what they are, my interest in girls soon overwhelmed my pride. By the time I graduated from high school I had dated most of the girls in our church's youth group. They probably were of the opinion that I was a nice fellow, but somewhat strange.

In college, however, the business of courtship became a serious matter since marriage was now a definite possibility. Mother had warned me to be very careful and had counseled me to ask the Lord to help me find the right girl. I determined to date only Christian girls, confident that I would recognize the right one when I saw her.

Within a month I was going steady. The courtship did not last long and was but the first in a series of short-lived romances bruising to both myself and the girls I dated. My problem was that if a girl wasn't a possibility for marriage, I wouldn't date her. If I started dating a girl and she dated someone else, I dropped her. It was all very intense.

Once the girls found out how serious I was, they wanted to know a bit more about me. When they found out that I was planning to become a doctor, the friendship warmed up. When they found out that I was planning to be a missionary doctor, the relationship either cooled on the spot or gradually unraveled. I became somewhat of a loner.

Finally, an attractive girl planning a career in missionary medicine began to show an interest in me. I became so convinced that she was God's choice for me that I didn't bother to ask the Lord. Six months later she explained that I was not the right man for her. My world collapsed. In the pain of the moment, I turned to the Lord for companionship and love. Once again I found that when I hurt the most, God healed the best.

For the first time in my life I began to seriously consider celibacy. Previously the idea had repelled me, but now, still feeling like a boxer the day after losing a big fight, I was ready to think about it. In my heart I hoped I would still find the girl of my dreams, but now I was willing just to do nothing. If there was a right one, God would bring her to me. If there wasn't, I could wait, perhaps forever. Two months later I rediscovered Becki Mitchell!

I was attending summer school and had already been accepted to the University of Pittsburgh School of Medicine for the fall semester of 1969. Because my younger brother, Dale, was returning to the States from Dalat School, I drove to New York to meet him. At my sister's house in Nyack I learned that one of my former classmates in Malaysia was getting married in a few weeks. We were all invited to a Dalat reunion party at the home of a retired missionary.

As far as parties go, it was pretty tame. The room was crowded and, after loading up my plate with cookies and soft drinks, I sat down in a corner to talk with some old friends. About half an hour into the evening I noticed a very attractive brunette sitting across the room. I thought, *This is supposed to be a Dalat school reunion, but I don't recognize that girl.*

I leaned over to my sister. "Who is that nice-looking girl?" I whispered. When she told me that it was Becki Mitchell, I laughed right out loud. A second look assured me that indeed it was Becki. What a difference five years had made!

She noticed me staring at her. I moved to the other side of the room and introduced myself. To my surprise she was friendly and even remembered me! As we talked, I learned that, despite all the years we had gone to Dalat school together, I really did not know her at all. She had opinions, intelligence and a charm that left me feeling warm all over! Forgotten were the days when she outran, outjumped, outclimbed and outplayed me. When it was time to go home, I regretfully said goodnight.

"It just doesn't seem fair," I complained to my sister as we got into the car. "The most interesting girl I've met in years goes to school in Tacoma, Washington while I go to school in Pittsburgh!" There was clearly no future in that.

I drove back to Pittsburgh with my brother, a maze of conflicting emotions running rampant through my mind. All week long I prayed about Becki Mitchell, asking the Lord to show me what to do next. By the end of the week I knew what I had to do—pursue her!

The following weekend I decided I should visit my sister again in Nyack. Surely Dale needed to see more of his sister—it seemed only natural! After a nine-hour drive, we arrived at 2 a.m. At 8 a.m. the next morning I dialed Becki's number. To my surprise she agreed to go out with me that night.

It was the beginning of a special friendship and a great romance. Having both lost missionary parents, Becki and I understood each other's feelings almost intuitively. We had both struggled, vainly trying to understand God's purpose, and both of us had finally ended up holding on to the admonition of Proverbs 3:5: "Trust in the LORD with all your heart and lean not on your own understanding." We had both learned that absolute trust in God does not preclude emotional suffering. Finally, we both had experienced a kind of unconfirmable loss—the ones we had loved were gone, but we had never personally seen the irrefutable evidence of their deaths. My parents and her dad had just sort of disappeared. The only difference was that I knew my parents were in heaven, while she still did not know if her father was dead or alive. As we shared our feelings, the powerful magnetism of common suffering bound us together. It became pure pleasure to drive eight hours—and pay the tolls—every weekend on the Pennsylvania turnpike.

In September we left for opposite ends of the North American continent, Becki to continue her nurse's training in Tacoma, and I to begin medical school in Pittsburgh. During Christmas break I had ten days off. A friend of mine wanted to go to California for the break, so we agreed to take his car and share the driving. I was put in charge of the food for the trip and since bologna was cheap, I made forty bologna sandwiches.

As soon as classes were out we started off, changing drivers every two hours. Instead of stopping to eat, we ate the bologna sandwiches I had prepared. At first they tasted pretty good, but by the second day we couldn't stand them. We reached Sacramento, California in forty-eight hours. Becki met me there, and we drove through beautiful snow-covered forests to Klamath Falls, Oregon to spend the holidays with her aunt and uncle.

Within two weeks of that first meeting in Nyack, I knew that I wanted to marry her. I was madly in love with her, and I thought she loved me; but would she marry me? It seemed a bit rash to ask so soon. *What if she turns me down? What will I do then?* It was a thought more terrifying than death.

Becki welcomed me so enthusiastically in Sacramento that I took heart. Two days after Christmas and the day before I had to leave, we climbed a hill overlooking Klamath Falls. Snowflakes were drifting down, camouflaging the city lights below in an almost make-believe glow. Alone on the hill, two people embraced. One was enjoying the romantic moment; one was terrified. I was at a crossroads in my life, and this girl had the power to crush me or to make me intoxicatingly happy. The only sound in that silent night was our breathing. I stopped breathing and asked her to marry me.

I had expected her to stop breathing too, either in shock or astonishment. Surely she would at least want to think about it for an hour or so. She might even want to think—no, pray—about it for a week. When she answered "yes" in the next breath, I nearly fainted.

"Are you sure?" I asked. "I mean, really?" I couldn't believe I had heard right. She was laughing at me. Of course she was sure! She had been sure of it since the night of the Dalat reunion in Nyack. That same night she had gone home and written her mother that she had met the man she was going to marry. She had been waiting for me the whole time!

After so many disappointments, I was afraid to believe that God could be so good to me. As the months passed and the letters and phone calls confirmed that her love for me was real, I began to see more clearly a side of God I had forgotten—His benevolence. I had seen Him surround His deeds in clouds of impenetrable mystery and I had heard Him demand trust and obedience. Now His goodness, love and kindness unfolded like the petals of a flower in bloom. He had miraculously provided for all of my financial needs. He had opened the high and forbidding gates to medical school, and now He had given me the bright promise that I would once again belong to someone.

On June 26, 1971 Becki and I were married. Six years later, we arrived in Gabon, West Africa.

Five

HOW TO RELOCATE A DISLOCATED KNEE

"There's a patient here who injured his knee last week," one of our African nurses announced one morning as I arrived at the Bongolo Hospital to begin the day. "He needs to see you."

I didn't think too much about it. Such events were not uncommon in this jungle enclave. I followed her to the outpatient clinic where a middle-aged man sat in considerable discomfort on a wooden bench. His knee was swollen to twice its normal size.

In answer to my questions, Mr. Mouloungui Aaron explained that he worked for a company that was clearing a path for high-voltage power lines through the rain forest. His job was to fell trees with a chain saw and cut them up so a bulldozer could push them into piles. A week earlier, while he was cutting a log, a section he had already sawed rolled toward him and smashed into his right knee. Since then he hadn't been able to stand up. It had taken him a week to get a ride out to a road and to our hospital.

The injured man's knee was not only swollen but his leg also appeared to be three to four inches shorter than the other one. The X ray showed that the blow had dislocated his knee but had not broken it. His leg was shorter because the head of his tibia was somewhere up in his posterior thigh.

As I explained that we would need to put his knee back into place in the operating room under anesthesia, I tried to look confident. I did not want to frighten him unnecessarily about the seriousness of his injury, especially since I wasn't sure how to fix it! Etienne, my surgical assistant, wheeled him over to the operating room.

Instead of going directly to the operating room I went to my office to look through my orthopedic textbooks. There I found several references to the problem of week-old knee dislocations. Words like "serious," "difficult," "nerve damage" and "arterial compromise" rolled somberly from the musty pages. It was clear that if I failed to relocate the man's knee, surgery would be the only remaining alternative.

The book's description of what I would have to do surgically to such a knee was even more sobering, especially since I remembered only about three of the twenty-seven anatomic structures described in the procedure! As I entered the operating room in my scrubs, the thought of evacuating the man to Libreville, the capital city, worked its way through my mind. There were three orthopedic surgeons in the country, all working in Libreville. To get to them, he would have to return to his village more than 100 kilometers away and pay the required caretaker and cook $100 to accompany him on the ride to Libreville in the back of an open pickup truck. Once there he would be one of maybe 100 patients with serious orthopedic injuries from all over the country.

I could see from his shabby clothes that Aaron had neither the money to travel to Libreville nor the luxury of waiting another two to three weeks to find the help he needed. I would simply have to ask God for another miracle.

As I pondered the options, the injured man, now dressed in a clean patient gown, lay hopefully on the table. He had no clue that I had never fixed a dislocated knee that had been out of place for a week. Etienne, my assistant, had already given him a spinal anesthetic, and for the first time in a week the man felt no pain.

"Here's what we're going to do," I said with far more confidence than I felt and squeezing his arm to reassure him of our good intentions. "We're going to try to put your knee back in place. It will not be easy, but God will help us." His face relaxed, and he smiled. Etienne then prayed, thanking God for the wisdom and skill He gave us each day in the operating room and asking Him to please help us again.

Because of the spinal anesthetic, Aaron could feel nothing below his hips. I had Etienne hold the injured man's right thigh above the knee while I grasped his calf and foot. I braced my feet and pulled very firmly. Nothing budged. Holding the calf and foot with even more determination and bracing one foot against the base of the OR table, I pulled until the veins in my face swelled and turned purple. The knee did not even move a quarter of an inch.

Undeterred, I told Etienne to hold Aaron's torso firmly, since I was about to unleash the full power of my arms, shoulders, upper torso and legs on the recalcitrant knee. I planted both feet on the base of the table, grasped the patient's calf like my life depended on it, took a deep breath and pulled with all my might. At the last possible moment, my strength overcame Etienne's. Had the patient not grabbed onto the sides of the table we all might have ended up on the floor.

A reexamination of the dislocated knee revealed no visible progress, with the exception of some red marks on his calf in the shape of my hands. While we caught our breath, I silently reminded the Lord that we needed some additional inspiration. A moment later it came to me: we needed to place a post into the OR table between his legs so that he couldn't slide off the end of the table when I pulled! We padded the metal post well, moved Aaron's privates out of the way (which he couldn't feel anyway) and tried again. Although I pulled until I saw spots in front of my eyes, the knee would not budge.

Once again we stopped and regrouped, and again God gave me an idea. My mind's eye pictured the winch on the front of my truck. That was it! We needed some kind of winch! After a moment of imagining pulleys and cables running into the OR building and around the halls and corners, I also remembered that I had up in my house a heavy-duty rachet tie-down for securing loads on the roof of my truck. If we were to attach one end of a rachet tie-down strap to the man's foot we could rachet the knee into place. But where would we attach the other end?

There was a second door into the operating room in the direction of the patient's foot. If we put a two-by-four across the outside of the door, attached one end of the strap to it and the other end to Aaron's foot, we would surely be able to pull the knee back into place. I slipped out the door and drove the half-mile from the hospital to my house, located the tie-down straps in our storeroom, dusted them off and headed back to the hospital.

In the meantime, Etienne had found a four-foot-long two-by-four. We tied one end of the strap around the patient's ankle with some cotton padding and the other end to the two-by-four braced crossways outside the door.

When everything was ready I began to ratchet. Moments later the strap grew taut and the foot began to move. Sensing victory, I continued to ratchet. The foot moved an inch! I ratcheted on and it moved four inches, six inches, twelve inches . . . twelve? When I stopped, I discovered that the dislocated knee looked the same. It was the OR table that had moved, leaving skid marks on the tile floor exactly twelve inches long.

Dismayed but not defeated, we detached the strap from the two-by-four and dragged the OR table back into place. On the next try, three fully grown men held the OR table in place while I ratcheted. As the sounds of grunts and straining bodies filled the air, I ratcheted the 500-pound OR table, its patient and three straining nurses across the floor. Obviously, we needed a better plan.

During all this, Aaron seemed only mildly interested in the proceedings. He dozed intermittently, apparently convinced that the outstanding surgical team at Bongolo was carrying out the usual recommended procedure for fixing dislocated knees.

The solution finally came to me. What I needed was not more and better muscles in the OR, but tables. If I placed two tables between the end of the operating table and the door with the two-by-four, the OR table couldn't move.

Within a few minutes, we had brought in the necessary furniture and were ready to begin. I ratcheted the strap until it grew rigidly taught. But, as the straps grew taut, the two wooden tables between the OR table and the door threatened to buckle upward! It occurred to me that if under the pressure they flew into the air, the OR table might catapult directly toward me, maybe even impaling me with the patient's foot. In the end, I sat a nurse on each of the two wooden tables.

When everyone was ready, I resumed ratcheting. The nylon strap tightened until the patient's ankle and toes turned a brownish purple. I prayed silently that the patient's foot would begin to move and not suddenly rip off.

Suddenly the foot moved! Inch by inch the patient's lower leg advanced toward me. The pulses in his foot remained strong, so I ratcheted until his injured leg looked a bit longer than the other one. Then I reached over the table and gently manipulated the knee until it made a squishy click and dropped back into place. We all cheered.

We applied a cylinder cast to Aaron's leg and knee, released the traction and sent him back to his room. After the anesthesia wore off, he complained about a huge bruise in his groin, but otherwise seemed OK.

That afternoon our hospital chaplain stopped in to see him, but the man showed no interest in learning about God. The chaplain stopped by the OR and asked me if I would speak to him about the Lord. I told him I'd be happy to do that. That evening before going home, I stopped by Aaron's room and checked his leg. The circulation in his foot looked normal.

So I said to him, "Aaron, God did something special for you today. You could have had terrible complications from what we did, but God protected you and helped us. Do you know that God cares about you and has made a way for all the wrongs you have ever done to be forgiven? He offers you the choice to become one of His own sons and to live with Him in heaven forever!"

Aaron looked away, embarrassed.

"Thanks, doctor," he mumbled. "I really appreciate what you did for me today. But I have my own religion."

I nodded sadly and gave him a friendly pat on his good leg.

"I'm glad we were able to help you," I said.

The next day, Aaron was up on crutches, and I sent him off to Libreville with a letter asking an orthopedic surgeon to see him as soon as possible.

He returned a month later and told us that he had never gone to Libreville because he didn't have enough money. I removed his cast and started him walking. About six months later, Aaron walked up to me without a limp and asked me if I remembered him. I don't remember faces very well, but when he showed me his knee, it all came back. Incredibly, it wasn't even swollen.

"I suppose you know," I reminded him, "that God made our efforts succeed that day we put your knee back in place because we prayed to Him. If He had not helped us, I don't think the things we tried would have succeeded. It was God who prevented you from having any complications." He nodded and smiled politely but clearly did not want me to continue. After we talked for a few minutes, he thanked me for helping him and sauntered off. The last I heard he was living the way he had lived before the accident, as though God had never done anything for him at all.

He left us more or less healed, but although he seemed to be just fine, in God's eyes he was quite dead. "As for you, you were dead in your transgressions and sins, in which you used to live when you followed the ways of this world and of the ruler of the kingdom of the air, the spirit who is now at work in those who are disobedient" (Ephesians 2:1-2).

Sometimes the funniest things turn out to be quite sad.

Chapter
Six

ALMOST CRISP

I love donated equipment because it's free. Well, almost free. I say almost because we still have to ship it to Africa from wherever we pick it up, and then we have to find a way to haul it 540 kilometers into the jungled heart of Gabon, mostly over dirt roads. That by itself can cost a small fortune. What I don't love about used donated equipment is its unpredictability.

Take, for example, our first X ray machine, a twenty milliamp M.A.S.H. unit that arrived in an unbelievably heavy metal trunk (which turned out to be lead-lined), a crate weighing close to 500 pounds, and a seven-foot-long, four-foot-wide, two-foot-thick steel box that seemed to be bolted to whatever surface it rested upon. The three-piece unit had been ripening for more than thirty years in various military and civil defense warehouses in the U.S. without ever being opened. Since we didn't own an X ray unit at the time, when someone offered it to us for free, we jumped at it.

Six months later, the X ray unit and about eight tons of other donated equipment and supplies arrived in the port of Libreville. The entire shipment was loaded onto a large truck with considerable difficulty and then driven to Bongolo, picking up a generous coating of dust along the way. A crew of ten Gabonese workers hired for the day slid the X ray crates and boxes out of the large truck into the back of a smaller pickup to transport them to the newly built X ray room. It was at this point that I decided to help.

Because little of what happened next was planned, it is difficult to describe what followed. But let me try. I and four other men shouted conflicting commands and pulled in opposing directions as the trunks and crate were dragged, dropped, set upside down, turned on one side, opened so half their contents fell out, righted and finally opened right side up and emptied. Because the heavy steel box contained the X ray table, it could not be opened until we got it inside the appropriate room.

Two missionaries and ten Gabonese men managed to drag the box out of the truck onto the ground and stand it on its side. Two teams were then chosen and assigned to opposite sides of the seven-foot, heavily weighted object. At my signal, the struggle to get the steel box through the door began. One team lifted its end before the other team was ready. When the other team was finally ready and lifted, the first team gave out and dropped its end. This happened several times, pinching fingers, eliciting spirited dialogue and firmly compacting the earth beneath the box.

On the fourth try, thanks to a chorus of coordinated shouts and grunts by the players, the two opposing teams managed to lift both ends simultaneously. The stronger team forced the weaker team back toward the X-ray door, where its members wedged solidly, unable either to lower their end or retreat. The shouts and grunts increased in volume as the stronger team fought to push the box into the X-ray room and the weaker team screamed alternatives.

When the pitch of the shouting had climbed one or two octaves higher than at the beginning, the impasse was broken. The two players who held the sides of the box on the weaker team were scraped off by the door frame, leaving me and one other workman—a sixty-four-year-old man with bilateral hernias and toothpick legs—holding up our end of the box. In the agony of defeat, I must have lost consciousness, because to this day I have no recollection of how the box ended up in the middle of the floor.

Sometime later we discovered that the box was upside down. When we finally got it right side up and opened it, we found a cleverly folded X-ray table and a telescoping arm to hold the X-ray tube. This ingenious mechanism slid on greased runners in two directions, which we unfortunately discovered at the expense of several bruised fingers. The entire unit had been designed to be opened and assembled in minutes. Six hours later we figured it out and had it more or less together.

It was several more days before I learned how to take X rays, something I had failed to pick up in medical school and residency. The army had cleverly coated the inside of the trunk containing the X ray controls with lead so that it could serve as a shield. Since the trunk stood only four feet high on end, whoever shot the X rays had to crouch behind it and shoot blindly.

It took several weeks of experimenting with it, as time permitted, to discover that a twenty milliampere X ray is great for taking pictures of safety pins and fingers. To x-ray things like arms, legs, torsos and heads, you need long time exposures. For example, to x-ray an adult's leg required an exposure lasting several seconds. To x-ray a patient's chest, I had to hold down the button for five or six seconds. Since almost none of my patients could hold their breath that long, the x-ray ended up taking a time exposure that included several excursions of the diaphragm, chest walls and heart. Not surprisingly, my blurred films could identify only the gravest abnormalities. A clear and focused X ray of the chest was a cause for serious concern.

I tried only once or twice to x-ray a man's abdomen. The exposure lasted eleven seconds, enough time for his contracting intestines to produce triple images.

Mercifully, the twenty milliamp X ray tube burned out after three years, saving everybody hours of time. Some years later, someone bought us a new, 100 milliamp X ray machine designed for use in the tropics that serves wonderfully to this day.

The unpredictability of older military equipment could also be dangerous. In 1996, the U.S. military donated to our hospital a forty-foot container of surplus medical equipment. Among the many useful items were four large steam autoclaves. Steam autoclaves sterilize whatever is put into them by using heat and steam under pressure. The heat for these particular autoclaves can be provided by either electricity or gasoline-fueled burners. Since by that time we had fairly reliable electricity, I set up one of the autoclaves in a room behind the operating rooms and asked our missionary maintenance man if he would hook it up to electricity. The electrical connection involved a three-phase current and drew 9,000 watts, the equivalent of about nine electric irons.

The autoclave worked beautifully for six months, but two weeks after our maintenance man returned to Canada, and before his replacement had arrived, a bolt of lightning during a thunderstorm burned out two of its heating coils. Fortunately, the U.S. army had thought of that possibility and had provided extra coils.

Changing the coils looked like a straightforward procedure, so I explained it to the hospital's African maintenance crew and went off to take care of several medical emergencies. If our maintenance workers did not succeed in getting the autoclave to work, we would soon run out of sterile instruments and packs. Although fixing the autoclave was important, I did not have a day to spend working with them to get it fixed.

When I came out of the operating room around 5 p.m. to see how they were doing, I could tell by the litter of parts, twisted coils and tools strewn about the floor that my crew had not succeeded in changing the coils.

The next morning I had them clean up the mess while I figured out what to do. Perhaps, I thought as I studied the manuals, it would be easier to use the backup gasoline burners that came with the autoclave than try to replace the heating coils.

I had always been taught that fire and gasoline are a dangerous and sometimes lethal combination, so I approached the heavy burner unit with skepticism. According to the manual, lighting it was not difficult. Despite my assurances, the women who worked in the sterilization room and who ran the steam autoclaves wanted nothing to do with the sterilizer while gasoline was burning underneath it. Faced with a possible mutiny, I decided to look for one-eyed Bernard, the second-most experienced African on the hospital maintenance crew.

Ever since Bernard had risked his life to kill a black mamba snake in the attic of the outpatient clinic, I had been his protector. He needed an influential protector because he worked in spurts of about two hours, after which he simply disappeared for the rest of the day. Toward the end of the day he would magically reappear, holding a hammer or some other tool and looking suspiciously well-rested, but always able to explain what he had been working hard at for the previous four hours.

On the day that he killed the black mamba, there was a near-riot in the outpatient clinic. A crowd of about 100 people were sitting in the outside waiting areas waiting to be consulted when the snake, probably disturbed by all the noise, poked its head out from under the eaves to investigate. The patients, who up until then had felt weak and sickly, suddenly found hidden reserves and stampeded in a screaming mob to a safe distance. I emerged from the operating room in an adjacent building at about 10 a.m. to find the outpatient building surrounded by a crowd of patients and staff standing no less than thirty feet from the building. Pastor Luc was there too and he had already called for the hospital maintenance crew to come and take care of the problem. Three of them eventually showed up. One of them was one-eyed Bernard holding a hammer. I explained what they already knew: one or several of them would have to climb up into the attic and kill the snake.

Two realities made this an extremely dangerous idea. The first was that the ceiling was made up of three-eighths-inch plywood nailed to two-by-fours peppered with wood bores and spaced three feet apart. The only way to walk around in the three-foot space above the ceiling was to balance on these weakened two-by-fours.

The second reality was that the black mamba is one of the deadliest snakes in the world, if not the deadliest. Its venom paralyzes its victims, and if it sinks its hollow fangs into a person's head or neck and injects its poison, the victim will die in less than four minutes. We had a small supply of antivenin at the hospital, but it would be tricky getting volunteers to climb up into the attic to rescue someone who had been bitten by a black mamba that was still in the vicinity. So I was very surprised when Bernard stepped forward to go after the mamba.

"I'll kill it," he said with a toothy grin. He chose a pointed machete and a five-foot-long steel rod as his weapons and climbed the ladder into the small, dark opening that led into the attic.

Several of us armed ourselves with machetes and took up positions on different sides of the building in case the snake should try to escape. I secretly hoped the snake would choose to fight Bernard!

For several minutes, we heard only the sound of Bernard grunting and sliding around on the weakened two-by-fours. He seemed to be having some trouble locating the snake. Five minutes passed, and our attention started to flag. The crowd began to relax, talking about other things.

Suddenly, we heard a shout, followed by the sound of a machete flailing against rafters. Too late I realized we had not cut the electrical power to the building. There were electrical wires running everywhere in the attic. The banging continued and moved down one side of the building. Bernard was apparently in hot pursuit of the snake. The clattering moved to a corner where the roof came down to meet the wall. Then there was silence.

One of Bernard's colleagues ran into the building and shouted up at Bernard to find out what was happening. Bernard shouted back that the snake had retreated beyond the reach of his machete. He was preparing to go after it with his steel rod. His voice sounded about an octave higher than normal.

The battle resumed abruptly with the crashing of steel against roofing tins. The snake must have counterattacked, because the steel rod popped through the thin roofing tins and into plain view well away from the corner before disappearing inside. It ripped through the roof twice more, three times. Since it did not seem to be the right time to admonish Bernard for putting so many holes in the roof, I bit my tongue and gripped my machete tighter. The other spectators were not so thoughtful, however. Though not one of them ventured closer than twenty feet, they showered Bernard with a chorus of advice.

"Go for his head, you dummy!" a two-eyed, muscular twenty-five-year-old man shouted from my right. I could just picture Bernard hearing his advice and deciding to leave off pounding the snake's tail.

The sounds of battle continued for one or two minutes more, then stopped. A moment later, Bernard threw down the body of an eight-foot black mamba. He had reduced its head to a pulpy red mass.

When he climbed down out of the attic, he was acclaimed as a hero. He received my enthusiastic thanks with a lop-sided grin and a shrug before going back to pushing the lawn mower around for an hour and then disappearing with his hammer. We should have given him a medal or held a special ceremony to honor his courage, but to this day I'm ashamed to admit that we didn't even buy him a Coke. Anyway, when I needed someone crazy enough to operate the pressurized gasoline burner for the steam autoclave, I naturally thought of Bernard.

The instructions for the burner gave not the slightest clue that the device was a potential bomb. Step one instructed us to pour unleaded gasoline into the five-liter tank. Since leaded gasoline is the only kind available in most of Africa, we used leaded. The instructions did not explain what would happen if you used leaded gasoline, but we decided not to worry about it and moved on to step two: pump air into the tank to pressurize it. Step three involved lighting a preburner to heat a tube through which pressurized gasoline had to flow to get to the main burner under the autoclave chamber. Step four required nerves of steel, because the operator had to open the valve to the main burner. When one opened the valve, a strange mist drifted up and hovered above the burner in a ghostly cloud. Why it did not immediately burst into flame from the preburner just inches away defied logical explanation, but if you lost your nerve and shut off

the burner you were doomed to repeat the process. If you perse-
vered until the cloud caught fire, however, you only lost your
eyebrows. Bernard quickly got the hang of it and agreed to operate the autoclave whenever he was needed—which over the
next two days was often. He looked a little funny without eyebrows, but we all soon got used to it.

The tenth day of autoclaving with the gas burner dawned
like any other day in Gabon—misty and humid. Our staff
met together every morning at 7:30 for a Bible study and
prayer and dispersed to begin work at 8 a.m. I made rounds
on my patients and went to the operating room to fix someone's hernia.

I had just finished the operation and was stripping off my
gloves when the OR circulating nurse ran gray-faced into the
room.

"Come quickly, doctor!" he cried. "The autoclave is on fire!" I
ran the twenty feet to the sterilization room and was stunned by
what I saw. The gas heater was lit and burning as usual, but
flaming gasoline was leaking from around the control valve.
Tongues of orange and yellow flame shot out from under the
autoclave and liquid fire dripped down onto the floor to join an
enlarging pool of burning gasoline.

The women from the sterilization room had fled and stood
crying outside the back door of the building. Bernard was
frozen in the doorway, unsure of what to do.

In that millisecond, a hundred thoughts flashed through
my mind. If we did nothing but protect ourselves, the entire
building with our three operating rooms, all our equipment
and all our instruments would probably burn. In the months
or years it might take to rebuild, we would have no way to
deal with the hundreds of surgical emergencies that ambu-
lances brought to our hospital. Many people would die.

On the other hand, if I ordered Bernard into the autoclave room to try to control the fire, it might explode and burn him horribly, perhaps even blinding his one remaining eye. And if I tried to control it, the same thing could happen to me.

An empty bucket sat on the floor two feet away. Shouting at Bernard to run and get a bucket of sand, I rushed to the sink and filled the bucket with water. The only way to keep the burner from exploding was to cool it down and shut it off. As I ran with the half-filled bucket into the autoclave room, I prayed a desperate prayer: "Whatever You decide for me, God, I put my trust in You. Only help me put out this fire." In that instant, a picture of myself burned from head to toe flashed through my mind. Then the water from my bucket hit the fire, and the burner gave off a roar of steam and flame.

The flames did not go out, but instead overflowed in rivers onto the floor under the autoclave. One of the women met me at the door with another bucket of water, and I heard the OR nurse shouting for Bernard to hurry with the sand. Before I threw the second bucket of water I grabbed a towel, wrapped it around my hands, and reaching through the flames grabbed the burner and slid it halfway out from under the autoclave. A third bucket of water nearly extinguished the flames. Seconds later Bernard arrived with the sand, threw it over everything and shut off the control valve.

Does courage give birth to courage? Of course. Does God protect us when we take great personal risks to save others? He does it all the time. Many of us are willing to take risks to please ourselves. But there are other risks that aren't so pleasing to us that God asks us to take to help others.

Don't get me wrong, though, I still love donated equipment!

Chapter
Seven

FORGIVEN!

She was feverish, crying and holding her abdomen in severe pain when I examined her in the emergency room. I concluded that Anne Marie had an abscess in one of her fallopian tubes. Since I believed that it was about to rupture, I took her to the operating room.

It was a Saturday morning during a holiday weekend, and most of the hospital staff had the day off. The two nurses who were usually on call for the operating room were off, and only one of the replacement nurses showed up when called. She had worked in the operating room only once before. Four of our five missionary nurses were also away, leaving me with no alternative but to ask the replacement nurse to circulate.

I still needed an assistant, so I walked around the hospital to find someone I could pull away from his or her assigned duties. We were short-staffed everywhere, so I finally drafted a first-year nursing student to be my surgical assistant. She had never been in the operating room before and was terrified, but after seeing Anne Marie crying in pain and hearing my assurances that I would show her what to do, she agreed to help.

I made a conscious effort to relax as I explained to my two assistants what one does in the operating room. We rolled Anne Marie into the OR on the gurney, slid her onto the table and positioned her for a spinal anesthetic. The circulating nurse didn't know where the blood pressure cuff or stethoscope were, so I found them for her. I set my OR assistant to scrubbing her hands and arms at the sink while I opened the surgery packs and washed the patient's back with disinfectant to prepare for the spinal anesthetic. The circulating nurse looked dazed when I explained how the table controls worked. So to keep my gloves sterile I manipulated the controls with my right knee and foot to raise and lower the table the way I wanted it.

Anne Marie was writhing in pain and would not lie still for the spinal. Eventually the circulating nurse understood how to hold the young woman in the fetal position until I got the spinal needle in her back and administered the anesthetic. As it began to work, her pain disappeared and she slept.

By this time, my assistant had scrubbed her brown hands and arms nearly pink. Since she didn't know how to dry her hands or put on a gown or gloves without contaminating herself, I made her stand in the middle of the floor with her hands and arms in the air until I could help her. Eventually I got us both gowned and gloved.

Nobody had remembered to shave the patient, so we waited another five minutes while the circulating nurse located a razor blade and shaved Anne Marie's abdomen to my satisfaction. While she was doing this, the IV ran out. After she finished shaving the patient, she hunted around for another bottle but couldn't find one.

I finally sent her out of the OR to try to find more IV bottles, scrubbed the patient's abdomen with disinfectant and draped her for surgery. About that time Anne Marie started looking pale and clammy, the blood pressure alarm went off, and the oxygen alarm clipped to her finger began chirping. I worked the controls to the OR table with my knee and foot and lowered the head of the table so that her head was lower than her feet. I was counting to ten for the third time and was on the verge of ripping my gown and gloves off to do things myself when the circulating nurse triumphantly returned with three full IV bottles. They had no hooks on them, so we waited another three minutes while she rigged up a halter out of rolled sheet bandages and hung one of the bottles on the IV pole. The needle had apparently been clogged.

Just then, the blood pressure alarm again sounded. My patient was in shock. Contaminating my gloves and robe, I quickly inserted a large IV needle into a vein in the patient's other arm while the circulating nurse tried in vain to reopen the original IV. Saline poured rapidly into Anne Marie's arm through the new IV, her blood pressure stabilized and my heart rate returned to normal. I changed into a sterile gown and put on a fresh pair of gloves.

The spinal anesthetic did not work as well as I had hoped, providing adequate anesthesia to only the lower half of Anne Marie's abdomen. Because of that, I made a low transverse incision well below her navel. My rookie assistant clutched the drapes and swayed a bit at the sight of blood spurting here and there, but managed to stay upright and hang onto the retractors I handed her.

The pelvic abscess had ruptured, and things were a bit messy. I had to pack a large abdominal compress into the abdomen to hold the intestines away from the uterus, ovaries and fallopian tubes. Because our anesthetic level was low, the patient reacted to my pushing her intestines around by vomiting. The circulating nurse got an emesis basin to Anne Marie's mouth thirty seconds too late, but at least the girl didn't inhale what she threw up.

To clean out the mess in her abdomen, I had to suction, pull, clamp, cut and tie. All this activity served to aggravate

Anne Marie's discomfort, and she began to moan and squirm on the table. When several loops of intestine popped out of the wound, my young assistant nearly fainted. I could have instructed an experienced circulating nurse to give an additional anesthetic intravenously, but the one I had did not know where anything was and I would have had to stop operating to help her. The only thing left to do was to finish and close the abdomen as quickly as possible.

I placed a drain into the cleaned-out abscess cavity and suctioned out the last bit of pus while Anne Marie howled and fought to get off the table. Struggling to avoid snagging the intestines that surged around my restraining hand, I finally managed to suture the abdominal cavity closed. By the time I taped on the wound dressing, Anne Marie had quieted down and my assistant had regained her color. I felt badly that my patient had experienced so much pain, but we had gotten her through.

For the first three days, Anne Marie did well. Her fever disappeared, her pain diminished, she got out of bed and walked around and she drank some liquids. I treated her with intravenous antibiotics and checked on her every day. But on the third day her temperature spiked to 105 degrees, and she complained of bloating. Her lower abdomen was again tender and swollen. A sick feeling settled in the pit of my stomach as I examined her.

An X ray of her abdomen revealed a ribbon-like irregular white streak in Anne Marie's lower pelvis. That confirmed my worst fears: she would need a second operation. Several hours later in the operating room, this time with an experienced OR crew, I removed the abdominal compress I had left in her abdomen during the first operation.

I left the operating room and showed Anne Marie's husband the compress I had just removed, now wrapped in a plastic bag.

"I left this compress in your wife's abdomen during her first operation," I explained. "That's why she didn't get better." The man looked at the bag in horror.

"Will she get better now?" he asked faintly. I assured him that she would. The relief on his face was wonderful.

"Thank you, doctor," he breathed, "thank you!"

He obviously didn't understand what had happened, so I explained it to him again, this time adding that we would not be charging him for his wife's second operation and that we would be refunding his money for the first operation. At that he blinked in surprise.

"Doctor, I can't take your money back!" he said quietly. I assured him he could, and that I wanted him to because I had caused his wife a serious complication. Thinking he needed some time to think about it, I told him I'd see him the next day.

The next morning I instructed the hospital cashier to refund the money the couple had paid for the first operation. About midway through the morning, the circulating nurse brought a message from the cashier—Anne Marie and her husband were very upset and wanted to see me as soon as possible. I was not surprised. They were finally understanding the seriousness of my error.

With a heavy heart I left the OR and headed to Anne Marie's room. She was sitting up on the bed talking to her husband when I entered. Her welcoming smile caught me off guard.

"Doctor!" she beamed. "I feel so much better today!"

I smiled nervously and glanced at her husband. He looked troubled. Then her smile faded.

"Doctor," she said, "we don't understand why you are doing this. The cashier came and tried to give our money back to us, but we refused." She paused and looked at her husband.

"We don't understand why you don't want to be our doctor anymore."

I took a deep breath and started in again, explaining that I could not accept their money after a blunder that had put her life in danger. At that, her husband interrupted.

"If you had not operated on Anne Marie in the first place, she would have died."

"I should have done better," I insisted. And then Anne Marie spoke the words that took my breath away.

"Doctor," she said gently, reaching out and touching my arm, "why are you so hard on yourself? Nobody's perfect!"

I was dumbfounded.

"The important thing is that she gets better, doctor," her husband added. "That's all we care about."

I could have told them that in my country a similar blunder would have cost me my reputation and my insurance company more than a million dollars, but I didn't. We weren't in my country; we were in theirs. When I finally found my voice, I thanked them for forgiving me and assured them that I would be their doctor as long as they wanted. To make them happy, I also agreed to keep the money they had paid for the first operation. Anne Marie recovered completely and went home a week later.

Undeserved kindness somehow seems more precious than any other kind. God calls it "grace."

Chapter
Eight

A STORY OF GRACE
(PART I)

The whole, heartbreaking tangle started out simply enough: a seventeen-year-old girl wearing a torn, dirty dress wandered into the hospital outpatient clinic wanting something to eat. She looked quite a bit younger than seventeen and was about six months pregnant. Her name, she explained to the nurses working there, was Cornelia, and she came from Yissinga, a village some fifteen miles away.

Cornelia may have been a seventeen-year-old physically, but her mind and emotions were about six. She was mentally retarded, willful, suspicious and completely alone. Our African staff made further inquiries and by the end of the day learned that Cornelia was the illegitimate child of a local congressman. He had, of course, long since disclaimed any responsibility for the girl. Cornelia's mother had five other children by four different men, and on the day that Cornelia showed up at the hospital her mother's youngest child was less than a year old.

In the hope that her family would eventually show up, pay for her prenatal care and delivery and help her, the nurses in the outpatient clinic sent Cornelia to the prenatal clinic where she was examined and registered without charge. The midwives encouraged the girl to return to her village until her next scheduled prenatal visit, but she refused. Instead, she took up residence in The Good Samaritan, a kind of motel with about twenty-five beds that the local church offered to outpatients who needed a place to stay. Cost? About $1 a week. To eat, she stole or begged food from the other patients.

Several days after her arrival, Cornelia had a grand mal seizure that lasted a full five minutes. She had had seizures for years, but her family had never brought her in for treatment. People from the girl's village told us that she had become increasingly difficult for her mother to manage and had received countless beatings. After she had gotten pregnant, her mother locked her in a room in the house for days at a time until the girl attempted to set the house on fire. At that, Cornelia's mother chased her away to fend for herself.

Nobody knew who had gotten the girl pregnant, but it was assumed that one of the village boys had either seduced her or raped her. How she had found her way to the hospital was a mystery, but most thought she had walked.

Out of compassion for her, our pediatrician, Dr. Deborah Walker, made the unpopular decision to give Cornelia a bed in her overcrowded pediatric ward. Once installed, Cornelia caused endless problems, stealing not only other patients' food, but also their belongings. The African ward nurses had not had any training on how to deal with a retarded child in a pregnant teenager's body and responded with what they knew by experience—threats and anger. Within days, the staff and the rest of the patients in the building were demanding that Cornelia be run out of town.

It was clear to Dr. Walker that Cornelia had never experienced love, so instead of throwing her out she decided to use her own money to buy the girl food. She explained to the African staff that Cornelia had to be treated like a six-year old child, not like a teenager, and that she needed love as much if not more than discipline. Day after day she spent time talking with Cornelia gently but firmly, explaining the rules for staying in the hospital.

When the ward nurses saw that Cornelia responded well to this approach, they followed Dr. Walker's example. A sort of truce was established.

In the meantime, Pastor Luc, our hospital administrator, sent repeated requests to Cornelia's mother, asking her to come or send a family member to take care of her daughter at the hospital. Her mother never responded. Fortunately, Cornelia's pregnancy progressed normally, her nutrition improved dramatically and, with regular medication, her seizures stopped. When she was at term, she went into labor without anyone from her family to help or encourage her.

Nobody slept that night in the maternity ward. Cornelia was unable to comprehend what was happening to her and fought the midwives, screaming at the top of her lungs until everyone was exhausted. In the middle of the night, she finally delivered a healthy baby girl.

The next day, Dr. Walker sent word to Cornelia's mother that her daughter had given birth to a child and that she needed to come take care of them. Once again, Cornelia's mother did not respond. She seemed to be saying by her silence that Cornelia and her new baby were the hospital's problem.

By this time, Cornelia had lived at the hospital for more than four months. Even though Dr. Walker provided her with food and the hospital treated her for free, Cornelia constantly pestered other missionaries and the African staff to give her money or food. When Cornelia's baby was a month old, we decided the time had come to return both mother and baby to her own village. Carolyn Thorsen, a missionary nurse and midwife, agreed to take Cornelia and her baby, loaded them into her car and drove to Yissinga.

When they arrived they found Cornelia's mother and grandmother. Neither of the women were pleased to see the girl. Arguing that they had no other members in their family and were unable to take care of Cornelia, they tried to refuse. Unmoved, Carolyn told them to shoulder the responsibility for their own family members and drove back to Bongolo alone. Patients and staff alike heaved a sigh of relief.

Three weeks later, Cornelia reappeared, holding a sickly two-month-old baby to her breast. Her baby was malnourished, covered with scabies and was suffering from diarrhea. Reluctantly, Dr. Walker hospitalized Cornelia and her daughter in the overcrowded pediatrics ward.

To no one's surprise, Cornelia was a terrible mother. When her baby cried she became frustrated, often slapping or pinching the baby in anger. The hospital staff had to intervene several times a day to protect the child.

At times, Cornelia would leave her baby on the bed and simply disappear. Whenever this happened the nurses fed the little girl and then tied her on their backs, carrying her around with them as they worked until Cornelia returned. Sometimes this went on for days. Slowly but surely, a bond began to grow between the nurses and Cornelia's little girl.

When Cornelia's baby was about five months old, someone began calling her "Grace." Up until then she had had no name, since Cornelia couldn't make up her mind. The name stuck. As the months passed and Grace became more active and demanding, Cornelia grew less and less able to cope with her. Several times a week the nurses had to rescue Grace from Cornelia's tantrums. Whenever this happened, Cornelia would fly into a rage, screaming, crying and hitting the nurses. Then she would run away. Hours later, she would come back disheveled, dirty and contrite. She would sit quietly as the nurses or Dr. Walker scolded her, forgave her and then talked to her about caring properly for Grace. When the staff saw she was calm and sorry, they would give Grace back to her.

Dr. Walker and the hospital chaplain spent hours talking to Cornelia about God. They explained that God loved her and wanted to help her. Little by little, their gentle explanations and assurances brought about changes. When Grace was six months old, Cornelia prayed a child's prayer with Dr. Walker. Asking God to forgive her for her sin, she invited Jesus Christ into her life. She still occasionally flew into rages and tantrums, but they occurred less and less frequently and did not last as long.

One evening, at the height of the rainy season, Cornelia went to the river to bathe and did not return. The next morning, Dr. Walker went with Pastor Luc to the river to look for her. They found only her sandals and clothes in a neat pile at the river's edge. There was no sign of Cornelia. Suspecting that she might have drowned, Pastor Luc sent word to her mother and grandmother that she had disappeared. He then hired several men in canoes to search for the girl, but the men found nothing. Two days later, a fisherman found her body downriver.

Her family never came to help look for her or to bury her. Our hospital maintenance men dug a grave, helped Pastor Luc and Dr. Walker wrap Cornelia's bloated body in a blanket and buried her after a simple graveside service. The only family that now seemed to care about her or her daughter was the hospital staff.

There are no orphanages in rural Gabon because up until recent times there have been no abandoned orphans. The extended family always takes in the children of its deceased members and raises them. So, when no one from Cornelia's family showed up to take Grace, we were surprised. Several weeks passed, and the nurses at the hospital continued to care for Grace, carrying her on their backs during the day and evening shifts and putting her to bed in the pediatrics ward at night. Dr. Walker provided Grace with all the baby food and clothing she needed. Although several of the nurses were childless and would have loved to adopt the little girl, they knew they could not take her home and make her one of their own children without Grace's family's prior consent.

The idea of a stranger outside the extended family adopting a child is not well accepted in Gabon. To many, it's the cultural equivalent of the precolonial practice of selling children captured in tribal wars to other tribes as slaves. As much as they would have liked to adopt her, none of the African nurses considered it a possibility.

Several weeks after Cornelia's death, her mother finally appeared at the hospital carrying a thin, sickly eight-month-old child on her back. She confronted Dr. Walker and told her that she had come to take her granddaughter back to Yissinga. By this time, the hospital staff had come to cherish little Grace, and they responded to Grace's grandmother with a tidal wave of anger and indignation. Dr. Walker finally called the poor woman into her office to talk with her.

"Since your daughter Cornelia is no longer here to breast-feed baby Grace, how are you going to feed her?" she asked. "She can't eat solid food yet, and your own child is looking too thin for you to try to breast-feed another child at the same time."

The woman shrugged.

"I can't afford to buy her formula," she said weakly.

"Then perhaps Grace should stay here with us until she can eat solid food. That way, we'll know she is well nourished. We'll give you a place to stay so you can stay here at the hos-

pital and help take care of her." At that, Grace's grandmother
shook her head.

"I can't do that," she insisted. "I have to go back to my village to take care of my other children and my house." She
paused and looked away. "I'll leave Grace here with you."

That was the end of the discussion. The next day she returned to Yissinga. We did not see her again for months.

Grace thrived on formula feedings and on all the love and
attention she got from the staff. She filled out, reached devel-
opmental markers ahead of schedule, smiled and laughed.
She grew into a beautiful and delightful child. It troubled all
of us, however, that living at the hospital she was passed
around like a sack of manioc. Worse, living in the pediatrics
ward, she was constantly exposed to all kinds of dangers.

She was sitting up on her own when her grandmother appeared again and announced that she was ready to take her
home. But when Dr. Walker questioned her, the woman still
had no idea how she was going to feed Grace while
breast-feeding her own child and caring for four other children, all without a husband's support. Even if Dr. Walker
were to give her formula and teach her how to mix it, without
boiled or filtered water or meticulous bottle and nipple sterilization, Grace's feedings would become hopelessly contami-
nated and give her chronic diarrhea. We had already seen
hundreds of children die from diarrhea and malnutrition because the grandmothers caring for their daughters' babies
were unable to keep the formula, bottles and nipples sterile.

Once again, Dr. Walker invited Grace's grandmother to
stay to help take care of the child at the hospital until she
could eat village food. But Grace's grandmother refused and
returned to her village, leaving her increasingly beautiful
granddaughter in our care.

Chapter

Nine

HOW I LEARNED
TO BUILD

The problem, explained Pastor Luc, was that the hospital's outhouses were full again. What, he asked, should we do about it? In the past we had always managed to talk a nearby missionary with construction know-how into building us one, but at the moment we were fresh out of willing volunteers. Neither was there anyone around we could hire who knew how to build something as complicated as a cement house suspended over a deep hole.

It couldn't be all that difficult, I thought, remembering how the last ones had been built. First, you dig a deep hole, then you build a stone or brick foundation around the edge of the hole, and finally you pour a steel reinforced concrete floor over it with a keyhole-shaped opening in the floor. Bricking up the walls and roofing the little house was something our local masons could do without much supervision.

With these thoughts in my mind, I shrugged and replied, "Where do you think we should build it?"

Pastor Luc already had a spot in mind. Since I was between operations, we walked down to look at it. The site he had chosen wasn't too far away and not so close that you'd be reminded of its presence every time the wind blew in the wrong direction. I picked up a nearby stick and traced a five-foot-by-five-foot square in the dirt.

"If you can find someone willing to dig," I explained, "that's how big I think the hole should be." Pastor Luc thought the size was perfect and went off to find someone to dig. That was the last I thought about it until five days later when I saw Pastor Luc again.

"How's the outhouse coming?" I asked. His eyebrows shot over the top of his glasses in surprise.

"I don't know," he said after a pause. "I thought you were in charge of this project!" The two of us hastened down to the site to see what, if anything, had been accomplished in five completely unsupervised workdays. On the way there, Pastor Luc explained that he had found a man named Pierre to dig the hole.

There was no sign of Pierre until we came to the edge of the hole and looked down. To our astonishment, we found a hole already eighteen feet deep and corkscrewing clockwise as it descended. To give himself more freedom with the pickax, Pierre had steadily enlarged the hole as he deepened it.

As our eyes adjusted to the dim light, we realized that the ground we were standing on tapered away into thin air about a yard below our feet. I couldn't help wondering where Pierre might have been had we checked on him after two weeks instead of one.

Two things were immediately clear: 1) The hole was deep enough, and 2) Pierre would have to match the top of the hole with the bottom to avoid a sudden and unpleasant cave-in sometime in the future. We instructed Pierre to enlarge the top of the hole and not to dig any deeper. He seemed relieved, probably because he was having to carry the dirt out of the hole on a ladder with a basket. Pastor Luc's enthusiastic ap-

proval of all my suggestions had the intended effect of pro-
moting me to the job of building supervisor.

When Pierre had finished matching the top of the hole
with the bottom, it was eighteen feet deep, eight feet across
and ten feet long. It seemed to be a pretty big hole for an outhouse, but since we couldn't very well fill it back in we decided to make it a double outhouse.

The next step was to find a mason and have him build a
foundation of rocks and cement around the edge. Everyone
we asked recommended Jean Claude, so we hired him for the
job at $1 an hour.

On his first day of work and before I went to the operating
room for the day's first operation, I explained to Jean Claude
what I wanted him to do. I thought I had made it very clear
that the foundation needed to be laid right around the edge of
the abyss. Jean Claude nodded the whole time I talked and
seemed to understand completely. When I came by several
hours later, I was shocked to discover that he had laid the
foundation a foot back from the edge of the hole. Now the
area of air we would have to cover with concrete measured ten
feet by twelve feet. We had gone from my original plan of
twenty-five square feet of outhouse floor to 120 square feet.

Seeing my furrowed brow, Jean Claude hastened to assure
me that this would not be a problem, providing I had enough
steel reinforcing rods and plywood to make the forms. I had
thought of neither, so the project ground to a halt for a
month while I ordered steel and plywood from Libreville and
found a way to get it to Bongolo.

After the steel and plywood arrived, Jean Claude explained
that he would need ten sacks of cement to pour the floor. It
seemed a bit optimistic, so just to be sure I bought fifteen,
along with two tons of coarse sand. Jean Claude had a couple

of his helpers break rocks into gravel with a hammer, and two weeks later he informed me that he was ready to pour.

He and two helpers then spent two more weeks framing up the floor, bracing the plywood so that it would hold the wet cement until it dried, and deciding exactly where the two openings in the floor should be. Toward the end of what seemed to me to be a lot of contemplation and very little work, my patience began to wear thin.

Jean Claude assured me that pouring concrete over large holes was not a simple matter. He then presented me with a small, rectangular frame made out of two-by-fours and asked me if it looked right for the openings we needed to leave in the outhouse floor. They looked fine to me, so I shrugged and told him to quit dragging it out and get on with the pour. We were paying his crew by the hour, and the price for our little project was starting to look ridiculous. Jean Claude assured me that his team would be ready to pour concrete the very next day.

The next day I was in the OR up to my elbows in someone's abdomen when Pastor Luc stuck his head in the door. He cleared his throat politely several times before I heard him and looked up from what I was doing.

"Uh . . . hello, doctor," he said uncertainly. "The mason is experiencing a minor problem. He needs more cement." I stopped operating and blinked at him over my mask. How could they have already used up fifteen sacks of cement on a floor ten feet by twelve? Pastor Luc explained that they would need another five sacks. As the building supervisor, I told him to go ahead and buy them.

An hour later, I emerged from the OR and headed for the construction site. I arrived just as the masons were putting the finishing touches on their slab. It took only one glance to see what had happened. As the masons had poured cement, the plywood underneath the slab had sagged down into the hole. The workmen compensated by pouring more and more cement to bring the level to the top of the forms.

It turned out that the middle of the slab where the plywood had sagged the most was no less than fifteen inches thick! It was a miracle that the whole thing had not collapsed into the hole. There was nothing to do but hope it held until the cement hardened. Jean Claude assured me that there really was nothing to worry about, and that when the cement dried, the floor would support at least ten tons! It didn't occur to me at the time to ask him why we would ever need a floor able to support ten tons.

The next day the floor was still there, so we breathed a prayer of thanks and considered the next phase—the walls. This went much better, and by the end of two weeks our two-room outhouse was bricked up and covered with a thin aluminum roof.

About this time, Norbert, our most trusted and experienced African nurse, called me aside and asked me if I had noticed how large the holes were in the outhouse floor. He seemed very disturbed, so we walked down to where the construction team was measuring the doors.

"First," he explained as we peered inside the still pristine facility, "the opening in the floor is so big a child could fall through it." At this, he and I and the two carpenters measuring the door all crowded in to peer down at the hole in the floor to picture such a ghastly event better.

"How would we ever get a child back out?" he asked. He was right, of course. We would never succeed in breaking through the fifteen inch steel-reinforced concrete floor to rescue someone. In my haste to complete the project in under six months I had carelessly agreed to a hole size without consulting an expert.

"Secondly," Norbert continued while straddling the hole, "it's so wide that you can't put your feet on both sides and squat without falling backward." There were some snickers from the carpenters. By this time, Jean Claude had appeared and hotly contested Norbert's remarks. Just to prove he was right, he tried to squat over the hole. To the group's delight, he fell backward into the hole and had to be helped up. When we all stopped laughing, Jean Claude suggested that we make the holes smaller, but we weren't quite sure how to accomplish that.

Several days later, Pastor Luc came up with the solution. Jean Claude would cement a porcelain flush toilet over each hole, and instead of a double outhouse we would have two modern bathrooms, each with plumbing.

Jean Claude and his crew spent the better part of two weeks pouring square bases on which to set the toilets, cementing the toilets on their bases over the holes and hanging the doors. He was so slow I could hardly stand it, but the alternative was to do the work myself. When he finally finished, we locked the doors and stopped work until we could find someone (other than myself) to do the plumbing.

A year later (yes, you read that right!), an American medical student named Ross McCordic came to our hospital for a six-week medical elective. The afternoons were often slow, so one day Ross asked if there wasn't something practical he could do. He would soon be a doctor, but he was so handy with electricity, mechanics and plumbing that I asked him to take on the project of bringing plumbing into the double bathroom we had begun building eighteen months before.

Ross suggested that as long as we were going to bring in water for toilets we should put in sinks. He did a masterful job, and within two weeks the bathrooms were finished and ready for use. At Ross' invitation, we all went down to see what a properly installed flush toilet could really do. Pastor Luc and I grinned like schoolboys as the water swirled noisily into the abyss beneath our feet. All that remained was to organize a proper inauguration and to decide who deserved to use the bathrooms.

It was mango season, that time of year when children are granted unlimited license to throw heavy objects into the air to knock mangoes to the ground. Up until then we had not noticed that a massive mango tree stood right next to the site we had chosen for our new bathrooms.

A few days after mango season opened, Pastor Luc called on me again. This time I had just finished rounding on all my patients. I could tell by the set of his jaw that something terrible had happened. He led me down to the bathrooms, opened the doors and pointed to the new roof. I was shocked to see a series of large, jagged holes in the roofing tins. It looked as though some of the children had used bricks to bring down their mangoes.

From the outset of the project we had constantly found ourselves at the mercy of forces well beyond our control. Pierre, Jean Claude, a great deal of money and my own ignorance had combined to produce two exorbitantly expensive Western bathrooms that mangoes, large rocks and children now threatened to reduce to rubble. If we were to save the project, there was only one solution: The mango tree had to go.

Africans have been cutting down trees with axes for centuries, so when I agreed with Pastor Luc that we should allow Pierre to cut down the tree, I felt a certain confidence that I could go back to taking care of sick people and leave the details to him. The next day, however, Pastor Luc found me again and called Pierre over to explain yet another problem.

"If we chop down the mango tree," Pierre said with an odd smirk, "it will fall onto the bathrooms." I walked with him over toward what was fast becoming the center of my universe. Sure enough, the heaviest branch of one of the largest mango trees I had ever seen would fall directly onto the building the moment we felled the tree.

After studying the branch for awhile, it occurred to me that if someone were to climb the tree and saw that particular branch off first, it might swing to the ground while still partially attached to the tree, thereby sparing the bathrooms. If that same person were to cut most of the larger branches on that side of the tree in the same way, the tree would become unbalanced and would fall away from the building when it was cut. Pastor Luc and Pierre both agreed that this was what had to be done. However, Pierre refused to climb the tree, claiming he was afraid of heights and had never seen it done.

A week later, Pastor Luc still had not found another worker willing to carry out the plan. Meanwhile, bricks and mangoes continued to rain down on the building each morning before the sun came up. Fearing that the bricks would eventually break our expensive sinks and toilets, I finally volunteered to do it myself.

The next Saturday, I climbed up into the tree on a ladder, clutching my fourteen-inch McCulloch chain saw. The main tree trunk was nearly three feet in diameter, and the lower branches were at least a foot thick where they came off the trunk. Once I got up into the branch I intended to cut, I found it difficult to stand or sit in a way that freed both hands at once. Nevertheless, I balanced as best as I could, fired up the chain saw and cut several large branches in the lower part of the tree, taking care to cut only partway through so the leafy end would swing down to the ground and away from the building.

One of the branches grazed a corner of the building, but did no serious damage. After I had spent two or three hours balancing, climbing, sawing and fighting ants, the tree seemed about ready to fall on its own.

The following Monday, I brought my ax for Pierre to use on the mango tree and went to make rounds. A couple of hours later, I was seeing patients in my office when Pierre's helper knocked on my door. Pierre apparently needed more advice.

A crowd of about 100 onlookers stood at a respectful distance from the tree. Using a technique I had never seen before, Pierre had chopped the trunk circumferentially, like a beaver. In the very center of the cut, about four inches of tree remained intact. Pierre looked worried.

"It won't fall," he said. "It's perfectly balanced." I could see why he didn't want to chop anymore. By now it was too late to show him how to cut a tree so that it falls where you want it or even to regret that I had assumed he knew how to fell a tree. Something had to be done before a storm came up and blew the tree the wrong way.

Ten years before, our missionaries had salvaged an abandoned Allis-Chalmers road grader and had fixed it up. We used it to keep the dirt roads on the mission station driveable. The grader had a large electric winch on the back end with 100 feet of steel cable wound onto a spool. It occurred to me that if we could attach the cable to the tree we could pull it with the road grader in the direction that we wanted it to fall.

I jumped in my car and drove up the hill to where the road grader was parked. I had had to learn how to use it to repair our roads just that year when our missionary maintenance man was away, so it took me only a few minutes to roll start it and drive it down to the hospital.

A murmur of admiration rippled through the crowd as I drove the machine onto the hospital grounds and parked fifty feet from the tree. Signaling for Pierre to come, I began unwinding the cable. He dragged one end until it was at the base of the tree. Now all we needed was for someone to climb the tree and attach the cable to the upper trunk or to an upper branch.

For some reason, none of the workmen wanted to do that, so I ended up throwing a weight attached to rope over an upper branch. Then we attached the cable to the rope and pulled the cable over the branch to hook it to itself. When all was ready, I climbed back into the driver's seat of the grader and motioned for Pierre to resume chopping. He seemed reassured by the cable and swung his ax with new vigor.

The road grader had six large, knobby tires, and the four back ones were connected to the drive train. The old machine weighed about two tons and had a large and powerful diesel engine. I put it in low gear and pulled steadily on the cable while Pierre continued to chop.

After five minutes of watching Pierre, I couldn't imagine what could be left to hold the tree up, so I revved the engine and gave a tremendous jerk. As the tree swayed toward me, a cheer went up from the crowd. I notched the accelerator up until the knobby tires were spinning and throwing up chunks of dirt. It was impossible! The tree should have come down behind me, but instead it hesitated. Then, like a giant spring, it recoiled, dragging the roaring grader backward. With a shuddering crash, the tree fell directly on top of the two new bathrooms.

The stunned silence that followed probably lasted only about five seconds, but it seemed to me more like sixty. I just couldn't believe it. I had reduced my first construction project—one that had taken eighteen months to complete—to rubble.

Later, we picked through the ruins and found several reasons for hope. The toilets and sinks had survived, the plumbing still worked, and best of all, the fifteen-inch-thick cement floor had withstood a direct blow by one of the tree's largest branches. Jean Claude pointed out with considerable pride that a lesser floor would have collapsed the entire building into the hole.

Two and a half years after I traced a five-by-five-foot square in the dirt, the bathrooms were opened to the public. Since the majority of our patients didn't know what to do with sit-down flush toilets, we ended up reserving them for our more educated patients. Later on that year, we tried again and in just three months built a genuine outhouse next to the first building.

Two years later, I successfully built the hospital's first administration building and a year later a twenty-seven-bed surgical ward. In the five years that followed, I built five more buildings.

Experience is a good teacher, but only to those willing to be humbled in her classrooms.

Chapter
Ten

THE STRIKE

J*anuary 31, Sunday.* I was writing a report on my computer one Sunday afternoon when a battered white pickup truck pulled up in front of the house. Four young men climbed out, came to our front door and introduced themselves as representatives from the Lebamba Strike Committee. I invited them in and seated them in the living room. As I filled their glasses with chilled Coke, they gazed at the African paintings on the walls, the pictures of our kids and the African fish zooming around our twenty-gallon aquarium.

After we had sipped our Cokes for a few minutes, they got down to business.

"Tomorrow morning the town will be shut down by a general strike," the oldest of them explained somberly. "All roads leading into and out of Lebamba will be barricaded. This has nothing to do with you. It's a community demonstration against the government's failure to keep its promises. We are angry that our leaders have diverted funds and have not kept their promises to build our town a water system, put in streetlights or add enough electrical poles so everyone can have electricity."

Becki was in Libreville and was due to fly into an airport two hours away from Bongolo on Monday, along with some American visitors. When I expressed my concern that they would not be allowed back into town during the strike, all four men assured me that there would be no problem. They would leave instructions at the barricades to let any of our missionaries or guests through. They also assured me that people needing urgent medical care would be allowed to come to the hospital.

After they left, I explained it all to the rest of the missionaries on the compound. Except for those who were planning to drive to Mouila to meet the plane on Monday, everyone agreed to remain on the mission and hospital compound until the strike was over.

Monday, February 1. The next morning, I spent a bit more time than usual in prayer, sensing that I could not afford to miss any of God's cues that day. When I came down to the hospital, I found about half of the usual number of patients. Instead of ten or twenty cars and taxis parked in the hospital parking lot, there were none.

I was in the middle of a major operation when the electricity went off. It was not unusual for the power to go off for five or ten minutes, so we continued working with the aid of a flashlight. Fifteen minutes later, the electricity was still off, we were beginning to struggle, the air in the OR was stifling and the flashlight was growing dim.

The maintenance crew had been working on installing a new backup generator the day before. When I called for the backup power, they came to the OR door and explained that the old generator had been disconnected, and the new one lacked a key part. Worse, our missionary mechanic and one of our doctors had gone to Mouila to meet the plane. Fortunately, we managed to complete the operation without harming the patient before the flashlight went completely dead.

When I emerged from the operating room, I was steaming—and not just because my scrubs were drenched with sweat. Everyone outside the OR seemed to know that our town's new masters had forced their way into the large government-owned hydroelectric plant across the river and had turned the power off.

Pastor Serge, our administrator, had already gone to talk to the strike leaders, so I asked two of the hospital maintenance workers and another missionary on our station to help me re-connect the old generator. The relic weighed more than a ton and was coated with a mixture of dirt and diesel fuel. We le-vered it up onto steel pipes and pushed it to where the wires to the hospital could reach it, filled it with fuel and were trying to figure out how to connect it up when the power came back on.

A few minutes later, the administrator drove up to the ga-rage to tell us that the strikers had agreed to maintain power to the hospital. Still upset that they had shown complete dis-regard for our patients, I showered, changed into clean scrubs and returned to the operating room.

Around 5 p.m., I got a call on the radio from Bob, our maintenance man. He and the doctor who had gone with him to Mouila had arrived at the barricade with Becki and our American visitors, but the young men at the barricade were refusing to let them through. Pastor Serge and I drove down to the edge of town where they were being held.

The barricade was made of about five small logs and some old oil drums. It would take very little effort to move the barricade out of the way. The three or four young men strutting defiantly in front of the cars were half drunk and looking for a fight. About ten or fifteen adolescent boys stood by admiring them.

I let Pastor Serge do the talking. He greeted the young men and reminded them that we had been promised the right to come and go freely. They scoffed at that and replied that no one would be allowed to cross their barricade. Bob, our doctor, Becki and our visitors would have to turn around, drive the two hours back to Mouila and stay there until the strike was over.

While the leader of the group was talking, five middle-aged women carrying heavily loaded baskets of bananas and manioc from their gardens walked past the cars and approached the barricade. The young men tried to stop them from crossing, but the muscular ladies shoved them aside and scolded them like children. Who did they think was going to feed them if they stopped their mamas from bringing food from the plantations? Were they planning to eat dirt? The women continued on their way, wondering aloud how any Gabonese woman could have produced such stupid offspring.

Serge and I thought it was wonderful, though we managed to stifle our smiles; but the exchange did little to serve our cause. When Serge again asked the young men what they wanted, they replied even more offensively than before. It was infuriating, but I managed to keep silent so Serge could continue talking. He refused to show that either their words or their manner offended him.

An old African proverb says it is foolish to offend the witch doctor. *Wouldn't these guys be worried,* I wondered to myself, *if later tonight one of them found himself in the operating room under my knife?* My fanciful train of thought was suddenly interrupted by a rebuke from God's Spirit. God was not amused by my imaginings, and I silently told Him I was sorry.

Eventually the young men offered to let the cars pass if Serge paid them $30. We could easily have overpowered them, but it did not seem to be God's way of solving the problem. For the sake of peace, we paid the money. As the cars drove through the barricade and Serge and I walked back to our car, I felt both shame and anger.

February 2, Tuesday. Sometime during the night, someone felled a tree across the road between the Bongolo bridge and the center of town. This made it impossible for anyone to drive to the hospital. A group of young men set up a road-block at the fallen tree and refused to allow even pedestrians to continue on to the hospital. That day, none of our scheduled elective surgery patients showed up.

There were patients already in the hospital who needed surgery, so that morning we did a diverting colostomy for a woman with rectal cancer, put a tube in a young boy with fluid in his chest and cleaned out an infected hip fracture. The stores in town all remained closed for a second day, and the only cars allowed on the roads were those used by the strike leaders.

During the night, a fourteen-year-old boy died in the pediatrics ward. The next morning, Serge walked the three miles to the center of Lebamba to try to get a message to the boy's father on the police radio. The man lived in a town eighty-five miles away. Serge waited for three hours before the police decided to tell him he couldn't use their radio. He walked back to the hydroelectric plant and got permission to use their radio. He eventually found out that the boy's father was out repairing a road grader and would not be home for another day.

By evening, the boy's body was beginning to decompose in the heat. Since the strikers would not allow us to drive to the town cemetery, we buried him next to the church. After the funeral, the young men at the barricade would not permit the boy's distraught mother to leave town, so she remained at the hospital with her two small children, mourning her son's death alone.

That same afternoon, the strike leaders drove up to the hospital and asked to see me. I came out of the operating room and found them waiting at the door. The leader asked me if I would give them either diesel fuel for their cars or motor oil for their chain saw. I wanted very much to give them a piece of my mind for all of the trouble they had caused our patients, but a small voice in my heart again prompted me to keep silent and to help them, even though I knew they would probably use whatever I gave them to cut down more trees for blockades.

I asked them to drive me up to my house where I had some motor oil in storage. As we drove away from the hospital, the young men in the back of the pickup shouted to the patients standing around, "We're kidnaping the doctor! We're kidnaping the doctor!" They howled and slapped their knees in hilarity at the cries of alarm their announcement produced. All I could manage in response to their joke was a weak smile.

On the way up the hill, the leader explained that they needed the fuel and oil for the chain saws they had commandeered. The local population had grumbled so much about the roadblocks in town they had decided to remove them and allow the stores to open. He added that they also wanted to make additional roadblocks on the roads leading out of town to frustrate anyone trying to reopen the roads by force. They were planning to cut the electrical power that evening to the town of Mouila, the provincial capital eighty-five miles away, as well as to Ndende, a smaller town twenty-five miles away.

When we got to the house, I told the strikers that I only had motor oil to give them. They seemed satisfied with my explanation and produced a two-liter container for me to fill. I wondered if my helpfulness would not come back to haunt me.

That night, the strikers cut the power to Ndende and Mouila. Since the community of Bongolo was also connected to the Ndende line, most of Bongolo spent the night without power. Fortunately, our mission and hospital compound had its own electrical power line from the hydroelectric plant across the river.

February 3, Wednesday. The day began calmly enough. I again felt the need to spend more time in prayer than usual at the beginning of the day and asked God for His protection and wisdom. It seemed that more than anything else God was teaching me to keep my mouth shut.

For the first time in two days, a small number of patients arrived in taxis and cars. I performed two eye operations and was preparing to do a C-section on a woman who had been in obstructed labor for twelve hours when the battered white pickup truck roared up the hospital driveway again and screeched to a halt in front of the administrator's office. In contrast to the previous visit, the strike leaders now seemed angry about something. They pushed their way into the administrator's office unannounced. A few minutes later, they stormed out and drove off.

After they left, Pastor Serge came out and explained to us that they had announced they were going to cut the electrical power to the hospital. Evidently a crowd of about 200 angry people from Bongolo had demonstrated in front of the strike headquarters that morning. The people from Bongolo were angry that they were the only ones in town deprived of electricity, so the strike leaders came up with a solution that seemed equitable: they would shut electrical power off for the entire town, including the hospital!

Serge asked the doctors how a prolonged electrical blackout would effect our patients. We explained that several premature babies were on oxygen. In the surgery ward, a small boy needed continuous chest suction from an electrical pump to keep his chest from filling up again with fluid. We had only four hours of diesel fuel in our backup generator. Once it shut down, we would not be able to take X rays, order laboratory tests or operate. After six hours without electrical power, we would lose our entire stock of vaccines. Serge again drove to the hydroelectric plant to talk to the plant's director.

We hurried up and completed the C-section in under twenty minutes. The baby had to be resuscitated with suction and oxygen but eventually came around. Ten minutes later the power went off.

The hospital had a smaller, fuel-efficient backup generator for the premature baby ward, but we could not put the boy with the draining chest tube in with the premature babies. We finally decided that, if the power went off, we would watch the boy closely. If he began to fail, we would start up the big generator and run it until there was no more fuel.

The director of the hydroelectric plant was a devout Christian. When Serge explained to him and to the strike leaders that we only had enough fuel in reserve for four hours and that several children might die during the night, he was aghast. He begged the strike leaders to allow his men to climb one of the main pylons and disconnect the high-tension power lines leading to Lebamba. That way he could shut off the town's electricity without disturbing the hospital. Besides, he argued, if people died as a direct result of the strikers' actions, wouldn't the relatives seek revenge? Wouldn't the government hold them responsible? What if the army or police showed up and some of the strikers were injured? If the operating rooms or emergency room were without power, how could the hospital help them? The more he talked, the more the strikers listened. In the end, they ordered him to disconnect the wires to Lebamba and restore power to the hospital.

That night, our hospital and compound were the only buildings with electricity in an area the size of Vermont. So we wouldn't irritate our neighbors, we turned off all our outside lights and covered our windows.

Earlier that same day, we talked on the satellite phone with a representative of the American Embassy and explained our situation. He wanted to know what, if anything, the U.S. government could do to help. I assured him that we were not in any danger (if I could keep my mouth shut) and did not want anyone to rescue us. However, if the government would send someone with clout to talk to the strikers, the uprising could probably be resolved peacefully. I told him that it troubled us that the strike was in its third day and not a single regional or federal government official had come to see what the strike was about.

That evening, Serge attended a meeting in town and learned that the local officials were ready to call off the strike the next day if the governor of the province would come and agree to urge the government to expedite their demands. Later that night, the town leaders sent a representative to Mouila to invite the governor to come for talks.

February 4, Thursday. As our staff met for prayer at the hospital at 7:30 that morning, the sounds of compromise were in the air. Many thanked God for protecting the hospital. Everyone thought the strike would be over by nightfall. But then the Mouila police arrived.

Around 8 a.m., a contingent of fifteen policemen arrived at the first of several barricades outside of town and cut them apart with chain saws. The young men guarding the barricades fled toward town. As the policemen took apart the next two barricades, a crowd of about thirty strikers massed behind the final barricade at a small wooden bridge. Expecting the young men to flee, the police stormed across the bridge with their clubs swinging. In the ensuing fight, one policeman was knocked unconscious and several others were severely beaten before retreating back across the bridge. The strikers then swarmed after the policemen and chased them into the woods. When they came to the parked police car, they broke all its windows and turned it on its side. Then they poured kerosene on the bridge and tried to burn it.

Fortunately, only part of the bridge burned. The police withdrew to a safe distance, sent their wounded back to Mouila in another car and waited for the governor.

When the governor arrived an hour later, the strikers were in a foul mood. They made him wait at the bridge for several hours before they let him cross alone on the part of the bridge that hadn't burned. The young men were still furious that the Mouila police had attacked them. Not surprisingly, the governor denied he had ordered them to break up the barricades and attack them. Nobody believed him, but because he remained cool, the crowd gradually grew calm. Speaking softly but with authority, he insisted that all of the barricades around the town be removed as a good faith gesture and that the electricity be restored before negotiations begin. This demand did not go well with the strikers and resulted in a stalemate. After several hours, the governor left, promising to get back in a day or two. He warned the strikers and town leaders that the federal government could decide at any moment to send the army in.

That afternoon Serge reported to us that, because of the fight at the bridge, the young bucks wanted the strike to continue indefinitely. A cloud of gloom settled over us. We had food supplies for about another week. Thanks to the strike leaders, most if not all, of the frozen food in Lebamba had spoiled.

February 5, Friday. The next morning, the town leaders and the strike organizers met and debated what to do. Cracks were starting to form between the young men who had served on the

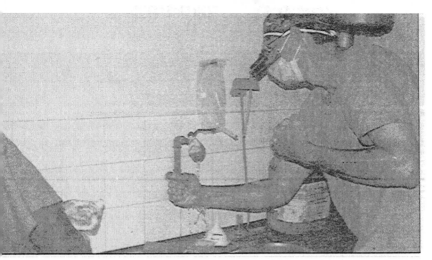

Since our arrival in 1977, the Bongolo Evangelical Hospital has grown m a dispensary to a full-service 100-bed hospital with a 29-month nursing :hool and a reading program in surgery. After scrubbing for five minutes, rinse with tap water, then gown and glove. After the "prep" pictured here, I removed a cataract from an elderly patient's eye. We perform about 100 eye operations a year on people who cannot afford to see an ophthalmologist in Libreville, 350 miles away.

Gabon has only three orthopedic surgeons, all working in the capital city. Before the hospital came, many children, such as the one pictured below, were permanently crippled from severely shortened or deformed legs following improper healing.

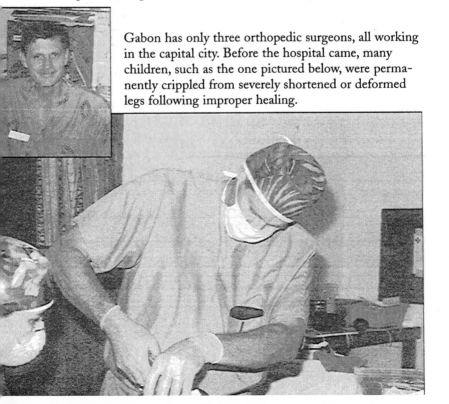

Our mission station, called Bongolo, is situated in the jungles
of Gabon, Central Africa, 350 miles from the capital city of Libreville.
Bongolo is part of the town of Lébamba, a community of 5,000 people.
The roar of nearby Bongolo Falls can be heard all over station.
Above: A view of the hospital grounds, now with paved roads.
The O.R. building is in the middle (behind the gazebo). The outpatient
clinic, lab, doctors' offices and surgery ward are on the right.
Below: A truckload of medical supplies has just arrived after 15 hours on
the road. The vehicle was donated to the hospital by Christians in Germany.

Our 20-acre station and hospital facility employs approximately 60 people, 50 in the hospital and 10 for maintenance. These four young men mow the lawns, maintain the mowers, and keep the power lines out of trees and the grounds looking like a botanical garden. Sili, second from right, is the hospital maintenance foreman.

We often have doctors who come for stays that range from a few months to as much as a year to fill in when our full-time doctors are on furlough. The Dutch medical student, shown here with some of our staff, spent four months at the hospital. "One-eyed Bernard" is far right with hat.

One of our nursing students, Raphael, weighs a newborn. Two shifts of nurses care for the hospitalized patients seven days a week, 24 hours a day and provide emergency services as well. All hospital patients bring their own bedding, food, pots, pans and firewood, as well as someone— usually a family member—to cook and do laundry for them.

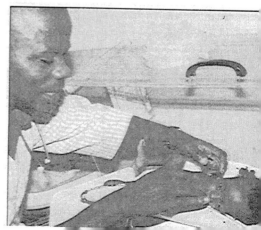

The Bongolo Church was the vision of a missionary named Donald Fairley who arrived in Gabon in 1930. Today, approximately 800 people gather in two churches in Lébamba each Sunday and during the week to hear God's Word.

We love donated equipment, but getting it here and getting it installed can sometimes be a labor of mammoth proportions. These pictures chronicle the arrival of the X-ray machine donated by a MASH Unit. (M.A.S.H. stands for Medical Army Surgical Hospital.)

Before the Bongolo bridge was built in 1995, everything—vehicles, people and supplies—came across the river on a hand—pulled ferry.

Unloading the X-ray machine.

This portable operating table never did look right, even after we got it put together!

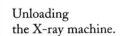

A quiet late afternoon at the hospital. The gazebo to the left is the social center and a place for our staff to catch a breath between emergencies.

The maternity building where our African midwives deliver 20–30 babies a month and care for premature babies. Note the church in the background.

The Bongolo Hospital sees approximately 100 persons per day, 15 of whom on the average will be hospitalized. Walk-in outpatients are first seen by nurse practitioners. Those who need to see a doctor are referred to one of our three staff physicians. Others are sent for lab tests (the window to the right), for X rays or to be admitted. All of our staff are believers.

With highways like National Highway #1–the road from Libreville
to Bongolo (350 miles),— you can understand that our vehicles
need to be four-wheel drives that are rugged and able to power
through deep mud and water.

In the rainy season–which lasts nearly eight months of the year–a
heavy-duty winch is one way to insure we'll arrive at our destination.

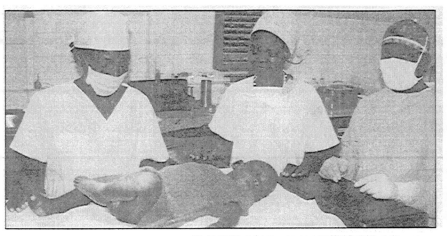

This child is waking up from a hernia operation. Since opening the hospital, we have trained over 160 nurses, some of whom now perform surgery, give general anesthesia, deliver babies and take X rays, among other things.

Above: This is the autoclave that caught fire. It sterilizes surgical packs by "cooking" them with steam heat under pressure.
Left: Baby Grace with Terry Hotalen.

Over the past 15 years, our midwives have cared for hundreds of premature babies, some as small as 800 grams (1.8 pounds). Such babies need careful tube feedings every 2-3 hours around the clock. Most have survived and are doing well. Before the hospital came, 95% of such children would have died.

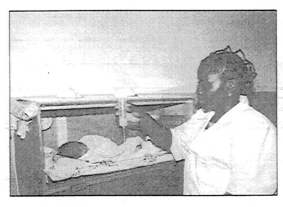

In 1993, the hospital sponsored a church plant in nearby Mackongonio. Becki is on the right, back row. **Below,** the elders of the church shake hands after the service.

Becki and David

This is the spacious and comfortable home of the Thompson family in Bongolo. It too was built by Donald Fairley in 1939 and overlooks the station. Our three children, Rachel, Joshua and Jeremy spent most of their childhood years here and are now grown.

front lines and the older men who had given them the green light. Not only did the younger men want to prolong the strike indefinitely, they also wanted to run a Malian family of shop-keepers and truckers out of town, supposedly because the Malians had refused to give them diesel fuel and had insulted them. In contrast to the Malians, they explained, Dr. Thompson had helped the strikers and had treated them with respect. Knowing the Malians as I did, I doubted the story was true. It smelled like either racism or revenge for some unrelated incident.

In the end, a deal was struck: the young men could run the Malian merchants out of town, and the strike would end for three months. If the government acted on the town's de-mands, things would remain peaceful. If not, the organizers would renew the strike "indefinitely."

The news that the strike was over reached us hours later. We were relieved that things would now return to normal, but we were saddened that the Malian merchants would be driven from town. It was the Malians who transported our medicines and construction supplies from Libreville in their trucks for less than we could do it ourselves. It was also the Malians who provided the majority of fresh food. By nightfall, the Malians had closed their stores and fled to the next town.

Keeping my mouth closed when I was angry was one of the wisest things I ever did. Sometime later, it occurred to me that God might have wanted more from me. Jesus said in Matthew 5:39-48,

> Do not resist an evil person. If someone strikes you on the right cheek, turn to him the other also. . . . If someone forces you to go one mile, go with him two miles. Give to the one who asks you, and do not turn away from the one who wants to borrow from you. . . .

> Love your enemies and pray for those who perse-
> cute you, that you may be sons of your Father in
> heaven. . . . If you love those who love you, what
> reward will you get? . . . Do not even pagans do
> that? Be perfect, therefore, as your heavenly Father
> is perfect.

The opportunity to love people, even when they are mean,
ungrateful or evil, is a gift from God that's not often appreci-
ated.

Eleven

THE ORPHAN
EVERYBODY WANTED
(GRACE, PART II)

After Grace's grandmother left the second time, several of our African nurses expressed their concern that she was prepared to take Grace forcibly even though she did not have a way to feed her adequately. At the same time, Terry Hotalen, a single missionary nurse assigned to Bongolo to work in Primary Health, was deeply troubled that Grace was growing up in a hospital environment instead of a stable home. After praying for the Lord's guidance, she volunteered to be Grace's foster mother until something acceptable could be worked out with Grace's family.

When Terry moved Grace in with her and her roommate, Karen Fitch, everyone breathed a sigh of relief. During the next six months, Grace learned to walk, swim and speak words in both French and English. Terry brought Grace down to the hospital several times a week to visit with her numerous "aunts" and "uncles." Every day she played with the other children her age on the mission compound. She soon blossomed into an inquisitive and affectionate child.

But everyone knew that the happy arrangement could not last for long. Even though Grace's grandmother was incapable of raising her, Gabonese tradition dictated that her family owned her and could not indefinitely be denied the right to take her back. It did not matter that her family had done nothing to help either Grace or her mother Cornelia over a period of eighteen months, or that the family was indirectly responsible for Cornelia's lonely death by neglect. Even the local Gabonese authorities were not sympathetic to the idea that someone outside the extended family adopt her. Our efforts to involve the local social service director fell on deaf ears.

By now, even the thought of turning the lovely little girl over to a family in Yissinga that would relegate her to a life of poverty and perhaps even prostitution was more than anyone at the hospital could bear. A wall of prayer rose to God on Grace's behalf.

Hearing that we were asking questions about Gabon's adoption laws, Grace's grandmother suddenly reappeared. She came directly to Terry Hotalen's door and demanded that Grace be turned over to her. When Terry refused and explained that the problem could not be settled that simply, the grandmother stood outside and screamed curses at Terry for several hours.

The next day, Pastor Luc called me over to his office and asked me to meet with Grace's extended family. *Where*, I wondered, *had all these relatives come from? Where had they been all this time?* Since Cornelia's first appearance, we had been told that the only family members in existence were Grace's grandmother and great-grandmother back in the village of Yissinga!

Pastor Luc's stuffy office now held one of Bongolo's chiefs, the local congressman (who was Grace's grandfather), a blind "uncle," another uncle who made a good living as a builder, and, of course, Grace's grandmother. The combined monthly income of this group exceeded Pastor Luc's and my salaries by several thousand dollars. Pastor Luc also asked Julienne, our head midwife, Dr. Walker and Terry Hotalen to attend the meeting.

Once we were seated, the discussion got underway. The first to speak his mind was the congressman. He thanked us for caring for Cornelia and went on to explain that since Grace's mother had had several lovers at the time he had known her, he could not be considered her father. Because Grace looked amazingly like him, no one believed him, but it didn't seem worth arguing about.

"Since in Gabonese tradition children belong to the maternal side of the family," he continued, "I cannot be obliged to take responsibility for either Grace or her mother. Nevertheless, out of the goodness of my heart, I am offering to pay all of the expenses Cornelia and Grace have incurred up to now."

I could have told him then that I had in my pocket a complete and up-to-date accounting of those expenses totaling $1,600, but since I doubted his sincerity, I decided to keep quiet. The congressman finished his statement by emphasizing his unequivocal opposition to anyone outside of the family adopting Grace.

This ignited the blind uncle we had never seen before. It turned out that he was a third or fourth cousin to Grace's grandmother. To our surprise, he launched into a passionate denunciation of our plans to sell Grace into slavery to recoup our losses. All of the other members of the family seemed to share this opinion except the congressman, who squirmed in his seat. As his voice rose, Dr. Walker, Terry and I fought to keep our composure. Pastor Luc listened as though he were carved in stone.

When everyone representing Grace's family had spoken, Pastor Luc blinked a few times and after a long pause explained that the only thing the hospital wanted was for Grace to be raised with a mother and a father who would care for her and love her. Couldn't the family find a couple in the local church that would be acceptable to everyone?

To this, Grace's grandmother replied that Grace was hers by right. She would not accept that Grace be given to anyone else to raise. This was more than Dr. Walker could handle. Trembling with suppressed anger, she left the room. After she left, I leaned forward in my chair and, looking directly at Grace's grandmother, made the point that since she had proven her inability to care for both Cornelia and Grace, as the medical director of the hospital I could never agree to let her take Grace and raise her. There was an audible gasp from the blind uncle. Grace's grandmother stood and left the meeting in a rage.

Over the next forty-five minutes, those who remained in the meeting agreed that the best solution might be for our midwife, Julienne, and her husband (who was somehow related to Grace's family), to take Grace and raise her as their own child, since they were childless. The meeting broke up more or less amicably.

Several weeks later, we were all surprised to hear that in a separate meeting with Pastor Luc, Grace's grandmother had agreed to the arrangement.

Chapter
Twelve

A TEST

In 1993, I accepted an invitation from the Christian Blind Mission to spend six weeks at the Ebolowa Presbyterian Hospital in southern Cameroon training in ophthalmic surgery. I had had a month of similar training in Zaire in 1981 and had learned a simple technique to remove cataracts, but I wanted to upgrade my skills so I could also perform operations for glaucoma and operate on eyelids scarred from leprosy.

The Ebolowa Presbyterian Hospital had been built between 1920 and 1950, and at the peak of its glory had a staff of five or six missionary doctors, a dentist, a nursing school and some 200 hospital beds. Its buildings were made of brick and mortar with glass windows, running water, electricity and linoleum floors. The operating rooms were spacious, well-lit, anciently but adequately equipped, and able to accommodate three to four surgical teams at a time.

In its heyday, one or two missionary surgeons supervised three to four teams of African nurse-surgeons operating simultaneously at the four tables. In the 1960s, the American Presbyterian Church turned the hospital over to the Presbyterian Church of Cameroon and withdrew most of its missionaries.

When I visited the hospital in 1987 it was ably directed by a dedicated Cameroonese general surgeon and ophthalmologist named Daniel Ety'ala. The eye clinic was directed by a

short-term Belgian ophthalmologist who was supported by
the Christian Blind Mission. It was his job to train me to perform three to four basic eye operations competently.

I quickly adapted to the routine at the eye clinic. African
ophthalmic nurses performed the initial eye examinations before sending the patients on to the doctors for further evalua-
tion. Three or four afternoons a week, the eye team operated
on patients who had surgically correctable disease. I worked
in the clinic and the operating room during the day and studied three to four hours each evening.

After three weeks, our team packed up our equipment,
loaded everything into a hospital van and headed north to a
smaller mission hospital for a three-day mobile clinic. During
the trip, I sat in the front seat of the van and talked with the
driver, a thirty-year-old hospital employee named Joseph. He
wanted to know why I was in Gabon and why I wanted to do
eye surgery. After awhile, we got onto the subject of my be-
liefs, and I told him that I loved God, was a follower of Jesus
and did my best to obey all that God teaches in the Bible.

The more we talked, the more irritated Joseph seemed to
get. It bothered him that I did not drink alcohol because I
didn't want to get drunk, dishonor God or cause others to
stumble. In response to a question about extramarital sex, I
told him that according to the Bible sex outside of marriage
displeases God and is harmful to those who practice it. When
I told him that I'd rather please God than be rich, he laughed
outright. He obviously thought I was just putting on an act.

Joseph's questions were initially couched in respectful
tones, but he soon let me know that anyone who believed
that the Bible was to be taken literally was naive. God created
the body for pleasure. To refuse to indulge those pleasures
was to contradict God's intent. I was struck by Joseph's com-

plete lack of fear of God. I loved God, and I feared His anger. Joseph had obviously never encountered God.

A few hours later, we arrived at an old mission hospital. Its condition shocked and saddened me. The ancient buildings were unpainted, leaking and in some cases falling down. Years of heavy rains had washed away so much dirt around the foundations that the buildings sat up on islands of dirt a foot higher than the rest of the grounds. The pitted and uneven cement floors in the wards were swept, but the overall appearance was that of decay. The weary metal beds wore mottled coats of chipped paint and the skimpy mattresses were deeply stained. There were few patients to be seen in either the wards or the outpatient clinic. The whole place seemed to be falling apart.

A tired-looking young doctor appeared and introduced himself as the hospital director. He gave the driver a key to the house in which our team would be staying and hurried off to take care of a problem in the operating room. Joseph drove the van up to the house, an old mission building about fifty yards from the hospital. Grass and weeds grew two feet high on all sides. Some kind of climbing vine had nearly enveloped one side of what had once been a large and beautiful home. My sense of gloom deepened. Was this what was going to become of my life's work in Bongolo in another twenty or thirty years?

We entered the front door and found the furniture and floors covered with a fine layer of dust. The once-polished hardwood was now scratched and dull with dirt. Carved, hardwood living room chairs sat in a room bare of any cushions, curtains, pictures or color. It was apparent that the house had once been a missionary family's home; now it looked more like a storeroom. Sweeping aside cobwebs we threw open the windows and carried our bags into the bedrooms.

There was no water, so Joseph went off to look for the doctor. An hour later, he returned with the news that the water would be turned on for one hour. Because electricity was so expensive, the hospital could only afford to pump water two hours a day. We took turns in the bathroom, standing in a rusting porcelain tub pouring cold water over ourselves with a pitcher. I was grateful that I had brought my own soap and toilet paper, but I had forgotten to bring a towel. I finally used my dirty shirt to dry off and changed into clean clothes.

By this time, it was 8 p.m. and we were hungry and ready to see the town. We climbed back into the van and headed into the center, a mile-long collection of dust-covered houses facing each other across a rutted, unpaved street. The hulks of abandoned and stripped cars lay every twenty feet or so on both sides of the road, shrouded in dust. In the eerie light of the headlights, the hanging dust and wrecked autos made the town look like it had taken a direct hit from an atomic bomb.

We stopped at several restaurants, but because the local economy was not doing well, every restaurant in town was already closed. For a while it looked like we would have to go to bed hungry.

Joseph, however, had hidden resources. Winding deep into the town's labyrinth of back streets, he stopped pedestrians and asked for directions. The third man he stopped apparently told him what he wanted to know, because he pulled away with a wave and drove directly to a modest, cement-block house. He walked over to a middle-aged woman standing at the front door and talked with her. A moment later, he motioned for us to join him.

We were so pleased that Joseph had found an open restaurant that we failed to ask him anything about it. We entered what seemed to be a private home. Two well-dressed young women greeted us at the door and ushered us into a spacious and well-furnished living room. There did not appear to be any tables in this restaurant, so we sat on comfortable over-stuffed chairs and sofas and watched an old French movie on a color TV that sat against the opposite wall.

The young ladies asked us what we would like to drink, and we ordered Cokes—except for Joseph who ordered a beer. The hostesses served us peanuts and refilled our glasses each time we emptied them. I couldn't help thinking that the service was extraordinarily good.

About thirty minutes after we arrived, the meal arrived. It smelled delicious and appeared to be chicken in a gravy sauce mixed with tomatoes and onions and served over rice. I know my chicken anatomy quite well, but as I gnawed on an odd-looking leg, I looked over at my ophthalmologist friend. He was looking hard at a lump of meat graced with several long whiskers. One of the African nurses with us noticed our perplexity.

"It's bush rat," she explained with a smile, as though she was describing spaghetti. After that, my friend left his piece of meat alone and ate his rice. I finished the meat I had and ate all my rice. As much as I hated to admit it, the bush rat was quite tasty.

About the time we were scraping the last forkful of rice off our plates, two middle-aged Cameroonese men entered the room. The young women greeted them so warmly that I assumed they were family. Our hosts escorted them to seats next to us in the living room, and the men greeted us casually. The young ladies served them glasses of wine, chatted with them for a few minutes and then turned to leave. Then the gentleman sitting next to me grabbed one of the girls by the hand and pulled her onto his lap. She giggled in a very unsisterly way and kissed him warmly on the mouth. The other man did exactly the same thing with the other girl.

I chanced a sidelong glance at my ophthalmologist friend. He was more a man of the world than I, but when I noticed a pink flush spreading up his neck, my worst fears were confirmed. We were eating in a brothel.

I glanced furtively at our four African nurses, but they were watching the television as though they had never seen one before. Eventually, they realized that the ophthalmologist and I were looking at them and looked over at us. We swung our gaze toward Joseph, who smiled and shrugged.

It was time to go, so we stood, thanked our hosts for the meal and paid the bill. As we drove back to the hospital, it was very quiet in the van. I finally asked Joseph why he had taken us to a brothel.

"What difference does it make?" he asked defensively. "We ate, didn't we?" He was right, of course, but it didn't make me feel any better.

The next day, our team set up in two rooms of the dilapidated outpatient clinic and examined about sixty people for various eye problems. We found six who needed surgery and scheduled them for the next day. Lunch was served at the doctor's house.

The doctor and his wife were Dutch and looked to be about twenty-five years old. Despite his youth, the doctor had a look of desperation and impending exhaustion about him. I asked him how it was that he was working there alone. He explained that he and his wife had been recruited in Holland by the Cameroonese Presbyterian Church to work at the hospital for two years as missionaries. The church had paid their airfare and had promised to pay them a monthly living allowance.

At this point, however, they had been there for nine months and were not sure how much longer they would be staying because, despite their best efforts, the hospital was not making enough money to pay their salary. For the past six months, their parents had been supporting them, sending money from Holland. I asked several leading questions but was unable to discern any evidence of faith in God. Their idea of what a missionary was and did was quite different from mine.

That afternoon, we finished up around 3 p.m. I went back to the house to rest while the others took care of the paperwork and visited old friends. There was a single sheet on my bed, so I lay down for a nap. I had just begun to doze when I heard a knock at the front door. When I opened it, I was surprised to see a very attractive young woman.

"Can I help you?" I asked. She smiled as though she knew me, looked away without saying anything for a few moments, then gave me a look that only an idiot could misunderstand.

"Joseph sent me here for you," she finally explained. I was dumbfounded, but managed to collect my wits enough to say that I was not interested. She looked disappointed and went off pouting. I was too angry to sleep, so I went for a walk.

An hour later, when I got back to the house, the girl was just emerging from Joseph's bedroom. She walked by me and out the door without a word. A moment later, Joseph emerged and followed her out the door.

Two days later, after we finished operating on our six patients, we drove back to the main hospital. During the first hour of the trip, Joseph was very quiet. Halfway home, he suddenly asked, "How can someone who is used to doing wrong things stop doing them?"

Unlike our conversation during the ride up, this time he really wanted to know. So, for the remainder of our trip, I explained as clearly as I could how someone can become a child of God through faith and obedience to Jesus Christ. To my delight, everyone in the car listened and asked questions.

A few weeks later, we went our separate ways. I never found out what Joseph eventually decided to do about Jesus Christ. What I did learn was that God always tests us about the things we say we believe. Psalm 111:10 says, "The fear of the LORD is the beginning of wisdom; all who follow his precepts have good understanding."

Chapter
Thirteen

THE MAYOR'S SOLUTION
(GRACE, PART III)

The agreement that Julienne and her husband would take Grace home and raise her as their child lasted all of two weeks. Julienne was suffering from a hernia and had to be scheduled for surgery the following week. She and Terry agreed that Grace would remain with Terry until Julienne had recovered from her surgery. The day that the mayor from Lebamba and the chief of police stormed angrily into Pastor Luc's office, Grace was still living with Terry.

"Where is Dr. Thompson?" he fairly shouted at Pastor Luc, standing in front of his desk without even greeting him. "I demand to talk to him immediately!"

Pastor Luc stood and politely asked the mayor to sit down while he found out where I was. But the mayor was too angry to sit. Instead, he stormed around the room while the Pastor went to look for me.

He found me in the middle of removing a cataract from someone's eye. Concentrating on what I was doing, I mumbled that I would come as soon as I finished the operation. When Pastor Luc explained this to the mayor, the man ordered us to appear at his office the next morning at 8 a.m. sharp. He did not specifically state what he was angry about, but we surmised that it had to do with a twenty-month old abandoned child named Grace.

The next morning, Pastor Luc, Terry Hotalen and I arrived at the mayor's office at precisely 8 a.m. We were surprised to find him sitting behind his desk in a suit and tie. In contrast to his demeanor the previous day, he was polite to the point of meekness. I surmised that someone had informed him that Pastor Luc's eldest son was his immediate superior in the Ministry of the Interior.

We chatted like old friends for about thirty minutes until Grace's grandmother and a young woman she introduced as her younger sister, Veronica, entered the office, accompanied by the chief of police. After everyone was seated, the meeting got underway.

Veronica and her husband, the mayor explained with a nervous smile, had agreed to take Grace and raise her as one of their own children. The couple lived in Franceville, Gabon's third-largest city about 600 kilometers to the east. They had four other children, a comfortable home and a good income since the husband held a well-paying government job. Veronica claimed that she regularly attended the Alliance Church in Franceville and was a believer. She very much wanted to resolve the impasse over Grace's future by adopting Grace and raising her as her own child.

When she finished, the mayor cleared his throat and explained that the reason he had come so suddenly to see us the day before was because the two women had sat in his office and wept over the injustice of their situation until he could bear it no longer. He hoped that by bringing us all together we could come up with a legal solution that would please everyone. Reassured by his conciliatory tone and by Veronica's evident maturity, we listened. The chief of police explained that if we agreed to this arrangement, he would write up a document that all of us could sign.

After a moment's silence, I expressed our concern that Grace's grandmother would simply demand that Veronica give Grace back to her once we turned her over. The mayor, the chief of police and the two women vowed that they would never allow this to happen. We looked at each other with questioning eyes. Could this be God's doing?

An hour later, the chief of police presented us with a document outlining the agreement. All of us signed our names to it.

To help Grace adjust to what would certainly be a painful separation and readjustment, Terry invited Veronica to come to her house to visit and play with Grace several hours a day until Grace felt comfortable with her. This seemed to go well, and after five days, Veronica took Grace with her and left for Franceville.

The separation was as traumatic for Grace and Terry as we had feared, but it seemed to be God's provision. Grace would now have a permanent home with a Christian mother and father who promised to love her and care for her as one of their own.

Or so we thought.

Chapter
Fourteen

DOCTOR:
MAN OR BEAST?

The dormitory at Bongolo's small elementary school for missionaries' children inherited Sheba from a missionary who loved to hunt. When Sheba's master was reassigned to the capital city, the dog was miserable, apparently longing for wide-open spaces and the hunt. Sheba's owner finally sent her to Bongolo where she could run to her heart's content.

There was only one slight problem: Sheba made puppies. Shari Timberlake, the dorm mother, did not want the added hassle of raising and trying to give away odd-looking, half-grown mongrel dogs every six months or so. She agreed to keep Sheba on the condition that Sheba be "fixed."

I had not the slightest desire to perform a hysterectomy on Sheba or on any other dog, so when Shari first asked if I would, I declined. Several years before, I had foolishly agreed to operate on a cocker spaniel that had a massive tear in the birth canal. The little dog had mated with a hulking village male dog, and the puppies she bore tore her bladder and left her incontinent.

I had rigged up an operating table on my back porch and put the trusting little dog to sleep with intravenous barbiturates. At the conclusion of one hour of surgery, the little dog's bladder and birth canal looked pretty good. I thought she

107

might do better with an indwelling catheter, but since I couldn't imagine what she would do dragging a urine bag behind her, I left the catheter to drain freely.

The postoperative care was a nightmare. The poor creature was incontinent of everything for two days and simply lay there in a pool of yellow and brown, looking at me. I cleaned her up several times a day and, on the third day, she finally stood and staggered out the door.

I was such a novice dog surgeon that I didn't even know how to keep her from pulling out her catheter and biting out her stitches. I tried everything I could think of to stop her, but by the sixth postoperative day she succeeded in removing everything, and the repair fell apart. At her owner's request, I put her to sleep, vowing never again to operate on animals.

Fortunately or unfortunately for Sheba, the memory of that experience had mellowed with time. The fact that Sheba was a winsome animal served to cloud my thinking even more. Whenever I approached the MK dorm, she would leap to her feet, give a soft howl of welcome and trot over to nuzzle my leg and look for a friendly scratch around the ears. Her sawed-off tail would wag until her spotted black and white hind end was a blur.

Her greatest talent, however, was hunting. The mere sight of a BB gun sent her into paroxysms of joy. Since most of the boys in the dormitory had BB guns and loved to stalk sparrows and lizards, on most days Sheba could be seen trying to run vertically up tree trunks, ineffectual but deliriously happy.

I never saw an animal as reckless as Sheba. Whenever one of our little hunters fired his BB gun in a particular direction, Sheba would fix her myopic gaze on some unknown object and point. Then she would leap through whatever was in her way in search of fallen prey. The boys rarely hit anything, but

Sheba's enthusiasm always made it seem like they had come reasonably close. Eventually, her zest for life wore away my resolve.

Jim Timberlake, the dorm father, agreed to help me set up a place for the operation. We dragged a wooden table into the middle of an open carport, swept it off and covered the floor with clean wood shavings. Since I did not have any intravenous barbiturates, I decided to use Ketamine, a well-known veterinary and human anesthetic that did not depress breathing.

We set up sterile surgery packs, instruments, disinfectant, sutures and gloves. Sheba was everywhere at once, poking her nose into my sterile packs, nuzzling my legs and making herself a complete nuisance. When we were finally ready, Jim ordered Sheba up onto the table. She hopped up and looked at us as if to say, "OK, where are the lizards?"

Jim helped me lay her on her side, tie soft cords around her paws, and secure them to the four corners of the table. As we worked she looked from one of us to the other with faint surprise. It would have softened a dog-hater's heart. I slipped an IV into a vein in her foreleg and injected a human-size doze of Ketamine. She relaxed in seconds and slept.

I had hoped that Jim would assist me throughout the operation, but as I shaved and prepared Sheba's abdomen, he disappeared around the corner. I put on sterile gloves, draped Sheba and made an eight-inch incision in her abdomen. About the time that I noticed the IV was no longer running, Sheba started to howl. She howled weakly at first, but then increased the volume and pitch to a wail that could be heard in every corner of the nearby dormitory. Jim bravely poked his head around the corner.

"What's going on?" he asked. "Isn't the anesthetic working?" Before I could answer, Sheba began thrashing around and got the paw with the IV needle in it free. I held a sterile towel over the incision to keep everything inside.

About this time, I had begun to perspire profusely. I needed to reestablish Sheba's IV, but if I took my hand off the towel over the abdominal incision her intestines would be everywhere. By now my neatly arranged sterile drapes were somewhere around one of Sheba's hind legs.

Our pediatrician arrived just then to save the day. Whether Sheba's howling had reached the hospital a quarter of a mile away or whether an angel had sent her just then, I never found out, but she quickly put on gloves, started another IV and gave Sheba another slug of Ketamine. Sheba relaxed again, and I replaced the drapes.

By now, Sheba had received as much anesthetic as we dared give, although we later found out that dogs require much higher doses of Ketamine than humans. She no longer resisted, but continued to whine pathetically. A group of teary-eyed bird hunters gathered just around the corner, peeking at us from time to time in anxious sympathy and asking if Sheba was going to live.

I don't remember what I told them, but, in the meantime, I had discovered that Sheba's reproductive organs were missing. I had a vague memory of canine reproductive anatomy from a course in Comparative Anatomy I had taken in college some twenty-five years earlier, but what I remembered was not at all what I saw.

For what seemed like an hour—although in reality it was only about five minutes—I groped around. I finally decided that the y-shaped, tubular thing running from her rear end to her neck was her uterus. I never did see anything that looked like an ovary.

To be certain that I was not about to remove Sheba's urinary system, I asked Dr. Walker for a second "expert" opinion. Her eyes glazed slightly as I pointed out a tangle of slippery, odd-looking organs. Her reply made me wonder if she would back me up if the case ever went to court.

Every truly great surgeon has one trait that is essential, and that is to be certain about what he decides. (This is secondary in importance to always being right.) When I was certain that I had properly identified the uterus, I removed it. Sheba responded by howling even louder. From the bird hunters around the corner of the garage, there came a soft, sniffling echo. Minutes after removing the uterus I had the abdomen closed.

Since my previous experience on dogs, I had found a book written by a veterinarian on "How to Care for Your Dog." Every fourth paragraph ended with the helpful statement, "Should this condition occur, call your veterinarian." Fortunately, the book demonstrated how to keep a dog from licking its wound or biting out its sutures. All it took was a big, cone-like collar. I had made one up out of stiff cardboard before the operation. After the operation Jim and the group of hunters dried their eyes and helped me place it around Sheba's neck.

Sheba survived the operation and apparently had no memory of my part in it. She produced urine in abundant quantities, proving that I had not inadvertently removed her kidneys, and by the end of the week was wanting to chase lizards. Everyone on the compound (who hadn't been watching) congratulated me for the fine piece of work I had done.

About six months later, Sheba went into heat and was rediscovered by many of her former canine boyfriends. Several of my colleagues expressed doubts about my understanding of reproductive anatomy and veterinary surgery. I was vindicated when Sheba failed to conceive and was even given credit for having developed a new technique that allows female dogs to live a more normal social life. Today, Sheba may be the only "fixed" dog in Africa that continuously makes you wonder if she's not.

In medicine and in life it is really important to be right, though, especially if someone's life depends on it. Confidence is not a substitute for knowledge, and sincerity will never take the place of truth.

Chapter

Fifteen

BETRAYED
(GRACE, PART IV)

Just a week after Grace left with her Aunt Veronica to live in Franceville, a patient from Mourembou, a village fifteen miles away, brought us the news that Grace and her aunt were staying in their village. This was especially troubling because the turnoff from the main highway to Yissinga is at Mourembou. Was Veronica going to break her promise and leave Grace with her grandmother?

Two weeks later, an evangelistic team from the Bongolo church preached at Yissinga and found Grace living in the village with her grandmother. Veronica had returned to Franceville without taking her. The news settled like a dark cloud over the hospital staff.

I was deeply troubled by the turn of events, so the following day I went to see the mayor. Had he and the chief of police been in on the deception too? If I was ever going to trust the mayor again, I had to know.

When I told the mayor that Grace was back in the village with her grandmother, he seemed genuinely surprised. He promised to ask the chief of police to investigate and report back. However, five days later Terry Hotalen talked to the chief of police, and he knew nothing about it. I again took off from work at the hospital to see the mayor, but he and the chief of police were away. I did not manage to see them again until a week later.

This time, the mayor had more news. The chief of police had hitched a ride to Yissinga and had found Grace in the care of a nine-year-old girl. All the adults in the house had gone to the forest to work on their gardens, leaving the children by themselves for the day. He reported that Grace was dirty and unclothed, but seemed to be in good health. The mayor asked me if Terry was prepared to take Grace back on a moment's notice if he went and got her. I assured him that she would gladly keep Grace until Veronica could return.

Since he had no car, the mayor asked if we could take him to Yissinga the following Sunday. He could not go sooner because a delegation of government ministers was due to arrive in Lebamba, and he would be tied up with them. I agreed to send Terry over to pick him up at 8 a.m. on Sunday in her car. But when Terry arrived in Lebamba on Sunday afternoon the mayor wasn't there. The visit to rescue Grace was again postponed.

Days dragged into weeks as more delays, excuses and missed appointments continued. It gradually became clear that the mayor had no intention of ever accompanying us to Yissinga to rescue Grace from her grandmother. The Christmas holidays came and went, and he finally sent word that his hands were tied. There was nothing he could do.

Had the family threatened him with sorcery? Had it become politically messy? He gave no explanation, but Pastor Luc thought that Grace's grandmother had probably threatened to use sorcery against anyone who interfered.

I was scheduled to leave in a few days on a month-long trip to the U.S. and Kenya, when one morning as I prayed I felt God directing me to go and confront Grace's grandmother.

The Saturday before I was to leave, Terry and I and the pastor of the Bongolo church made the trip to Yissinga.

When we pulled into the village, a crowd of about fifty people quickly gathered around the car. Many who came and greeted us were Christians or patients we had treated at the hospital. None of them expressed animosity when we asked where Grace lived with her grandmother. Several pointed out the house and smiled knowingly as we headed toward it.

The house was similar to most of the houses in the village, except smaller and more crooked. It was built of thin, hand-hewn softwood boards nailed to a framework of vertical hardwood poles and was covered by a rusting corrugated roof.

Grace's great-grandmother emerged from the house and greeted us suspiciously. After we explained that we had come to talk to her family about Grace, she turned and motioned brusquely for us to come into the house. We had to duck to get under the five-foot high doorway. Once inside, my head touched the low exposed rafters. The central room of the house was about six feet wide and ten feet long, with narrow bedroom doors opening onto each side. The floor was of packed earth, slanted and uneven. A wobbly table was the only piece of furniture. Someone brought three chairs for us to sit on.

Within minutes, more than twenty people had crowded into the tiny house. The only window, a two-foot square next to the door, was open. Two or three people leaned through it, while others who could not get inside stood in the doorway. The room was stifling, and everyone seemed to be talking at once.

A few minutes later, Grace's grandmother pushed into the room with Grace on her hip. She had awakened Grace from a nap, and the little girl was groggy. My heart sank when I saw how dirty and disheveled she was. Her left thigh was swollen and reddened with what appeared to be a large boil. When she saw Terry, she burst into angry tears and clung tightly to her grandmother. Terry bit her lip and fought back tears. She tried to talk to her and gently stroked her leg, but Grace only cried harder and refused to look at her.

In the midst of this cacophony of sound, the local pastor motioned for silence and began to explain why we had come. After a moment, he indicated it was my turn to speak. I added to what the pastor had already said, explaining that we were very disappointed at what Grace's grandmother had done. We had trusted her, but she had lied not only to us, but also to the mayor and to the chief of police. As I talked, a murmur of dissent spread around the room.

When I stopped, all heads turned to hear what Grace's grandmother would say. She shifted Grace to her other hip.

"I did not break my promise," she said defiantly. "The problem was Veronica's husband. He refused to take Grace with him, so I had no choice but to bring her back here!" I looked at Terry, and she shook her head in disbelief.

About then, a middle-aged man smelling strongly of alcohol crowded into the center of the room. Swaying slightly, he introduced himself as yet another of Grace's uncles. I found it hard to cover my amazement that little Grace had suddenly become the cherished object of such a large and adoring family.

In a rambling and convoluted speech that went on for ten minutes, Grace's newest uncle lent his support to the grandmother's assertion that she had been obliged to bring Grace to her home. Then he launched into a discussion of why he thought Veronica and her husband should not have custody of the child. To everyone's surprise, he concluded by saying that the missionaries should take care of Grace so there would be peace between the hospital and the village of Yissinga! A chorus of dissent arose in the crowd.

When Grace's grandmother motioned that she wanted to speak, everyone quieted down again.

"You can talk all you want," she said as she hung tightly onto Grace, "but I'm never going to give up this child to you or anybody else."

It was about 100 degrees in the airless room. I could feel the heat from the sun radiating through the roofing tins a few feet above our heads. Perspiration dripped off our faces and down onto our clothes. Looking at Grace with obvious compassion, Terry spoke to the crowd for the first time.

"What you are doing to this little girl is wrong. You made a promise to us, to the mayor and to the chief of police that you would give Grace to Veronica and her husband, relatives of yours who have the means to take care of her, love her, teach her about God and give her a good education. Instead of keeping your promise, you have deceived us." When she stopped, she was close to tears.

The pastor added a final word. "You can deceive men, but you cannot deceive God. He will have the last word in this matter." In the uneasy silence that followed, the people looked at each other and at Grace. The meeting was over and there was nothing more we could do but trust God and leave. After we went outside, I approached Grace's grandmother one last time.

"I'm disappointed that you are not interested in what's best for Grace. For you, this has become a matter of winning, not of love."

She shook her head. "She belongs to me, not you, and I'm doing what's best for her!"

"No," I said. "If you loved her more than you love yourself you would give her to your sister and her husband to raise. You may get your way, but you are opposing God. If you insist on doing it your way and this child dies of neglect, you will be responsible for her death."

She glared at me as we walked back to the car. Grace raised her head and glued her gaze on Terry until the car drove away.

Chapter
Sixteen

THE GOAT'S REVENGE

Up until Ilobo asked me to take him with me on my trip to Libreville, I had only one other passenger, Pastor Luc. Ilobo was an old friend, a man who had been an elder in the Bongolo church for thirty years before retiring, and one of Bongolo's first Christians. His wife of forty-five years had worked as a cleaning woman at the hospital until dying of bone cancer two years before. Ilobo had loved her deeply and only now was beginning to smile again.

Following their mother's death, Ilobo's five or six children in Libreville had done everything possible to comfort their father and care for him. He had hardly noticed it then, but now he wanted to do something to thank them by taking them a goat for a family celebration.

I hesitated for almost a minute when he asked me if he could bring it along, but in the end, friendship won out. Perhaps I could tie the animal up on the roof where it could bleat and mess to its heart's content and not bother us below in the air-conditioned cabin. When I agreed, Ilobo's old face glowed with pleasure. He readily accepted my one condition that someone from his house tie the goat up on the roof rack when I came to pick him up in the morning.

The first hint of trouble appeared as I drove up to his house in the dim light before sunrise. As I got out of my truck, one of his nephews was trying to tie the goat's feet together with the same stiff piece of vine that was tied around its neck. After he had finished, it took less than a minute for the goat to free its legs from the vine and stand up. Ilobo's daughter, Christine, went and got a rope, and this time the young man succeeded in tying the goat's feet securely. For added measure, he stuffed the goat's body into an old rice sack, leaving only its head and neck sticking out.

This must be the way to do it, I thought admiringly.

Another nephew dragged two 100-pound sacks of manioc to the car and loaded them up on the roof with the goat. I was not satisfied with the way he was tying the sacks on the roof, so I climbed up to help him. To make sure that the goat would not bounce out of the roof rack I tied a rope loosely around its neck and secured it to the railing.

Ilobo got in and I drove a few houses further to pick up Pastor Luc. He brought out two more sacks of manioc which we added to the load already up on the roof. Our last passenger was Jim, a Peace Corps volunteer who worked in area villages teaching people how to raise fish in ponds.

The road was unpaved and rough, so we could drive only twenty or thirty miles an hour. The log bridges, blind curves and sudden mud holes kept me so busy I soon forgot about the goat.

An hour into the trip, we heard a sudden thrashing and banging against a back window on the right side of the truck. To our surprise, the goat was hanging down from the roof. By the time I got out of the car and over to it, the animal looked nearly dead.

Over the years, I had personally masterminded the extermination of more than 100 of these unsanitary creatures from the hospital grounds where they had insisted on living. But, at that moment, it only irritated me that one of them was trying to hang itself on my car. I climbed up onto the roof and manhandled the unresisting animal back through the narrow gap between the side rails of the roof rack. It lay there gasping, its eyes closed, looking more dead than alive. As it recovered, I noticed that it had made a complete hash of everything on the roof. Ropes, sacks of manioc, the bag they had tied him in and his choke rope were impossibly tangled and smeared with a sticky green slime that could only have come from him.

It took me fifteen minutes to untie all the ropes, pile the manioc toward the front of the roof, lash the goat's feet together and strap everything down again. When I was finished, the green slime covered my hands, forearms, elbows, knees and shoes. I found a mud puddle in the middle of the road and washed off as best as I could.

As I climbed into the driver's seat, Ilobo wisely chose not to ask what I had been doing up on the roof with his goat or why I had washed myself off in a mud puddle. An hour later, we arrived in Mouila, the provincial capital.

Pastor Luc and I needed to talk to the work inspector in Mouila about an employee problem, so we drove to his office, parked the vehicle and went inside. The meeting took longer than expected and would have gone on longer had his secretary not come running in to announce that the goat up on top of our truck appeared to be dying.

We emerged from the inspector's office to find four or five Gabonese trying to save Ilobo's goat! The animal had worked itself over to the left side of the roof rack and in so doing had tightened the rope around its neck until it was strangling. Strands of gooey saliva ran from its blue tongue down the windows of my truck. A man waiting to file a complaint against his employer was tenderly loosening the rope around the goat's neck. His employer was preparing to back my truck into the shade of a nearby tree where it was cooler.

Meanwhile, the inspector's secretary stood on tiptoes trying to give the unconscious animal a drink from a cup without getting saliva on herself. Overall it was one of the most astonishing scenes I have ever witnessed.

Embarrassed, we thanked the inspector, thanked the goat's rescuers, promised to improve the animal's traveling conditions and drove away as quickly as possible. As we bumped through town, I suggested to Ilobo that since his goat seemed determined to die up on the roof, perhaps it would be better to leave it in Mouila with the local pastor until he found a better way to get it to Libreville.

"It's only meat," Ilobo replied with surprise. "If it dies, we'll eat it tonight when we get to Libreville." My years of experience with goats at the hospital had drained me of all compassion for the creatures, but the thought of killing one by slow torture made me feel like a war criminal. And yet, if I untied its feet, I knew it would leap off the roof again. Perhaps once we got moving the wind would cool it down.

When I stopped just outside of town to see how the goat was doing, it seemed to be recovering, so we continued on. For the next two hours, the challenges of simply staying on the road once again displaced the creature from my thoughts.

We were about halfway to Libreville and rounding a curve when we saw a line of orange cones across the road indicating a police check. As we pulled to a stop, two officers sitting on chairs under a palm tree turned their heads toward us in slow motion. In perfect unison, their mouths opened and their right arms lifted into the air. As if they had practiced, their fingers pointed to the roof of the truck. Even from twenty feet away we could read their lips as they shouted, "Your goat is falling off!" Sure enough, when we jerked around and looked to the right rear window, we could perceive the dark blob of a strangling goat.

My heart sinking, I jumped from the car and ran to help. Somehow the goat had once again managed to squeeze its ten-inch thick abdomen and torso through the six-inch space between the top and bottom side rails of the roof rack. Since I had removed the neck rope in Mouila, it now hung not by its neck, but by its feet. Since it did not appear to be breathing, I was certain that this time I had finished it off. Jim, the Peace Corps volunteer, joined me just then, and while I pulled from above, he pushed from below, squeezing the goat back through the bars. The maneuver must have been therapeutic, because the goat lay on the roof and gasped like a fish out of water. Once again, I stood there looking at its blue tongue, feeling like a Nazi.

Fortunately for us, the police officers seemed to think our technique of transporting goats was more amusing than criminal. To the sound of their guffaws, I was allowed to slink back to my car and drive on.

We were hungry, so after refueling in Lambaréné we drove to a favorite fast-food restaurant next to a river and ordered omelette sandwiches on French bread. Jim and I untied the goat and gently lowered him onto the long grass beside the car. We freed its feet, tied a noose around its neck and secured the leash to the rear bumper of the car.

For the first few minutes, the goat just lay there, looking up at the sky with one dull eye. I wondered if it didn't have hypoxic brain damage. Feeling sorry for it, I climbed down the riverbank and filled an old can with water. I brought it up and offered it to the goat. It didn't respond, so I poured the water on its nose. At that, it jumped to its feet, shook itself once and started to chomp on the grass by the car as though it hadn't eaten in days. I tried to offer it water again, but it turned away in disgust and ate more grass.

The goat's resurrection from near death was so remarkable that old Ilobo climbed out of the car to watch it eat. When our sandwiches came, we sat in the car and ate them. I tried not to think about why my hands, clothes, shoes and even the inside of the truck now smelled like goat manure.

After the meal, the goat was so frisky that Jim and I ended up having to tackle it so we could tie it up again and get it back on the roof. This time we tied it so that it couldn't get even close to the side bars of the roof rack.

The trip between Lambaréné and Libreville takes three and a half hours over a well-paved but winding road. An hour from Libreville, we were engulfed in a heavy rainstorm. I thought the rain might wash things up a bit, but it produced only a sticky green film that drooled off the roof onto the sides and windows of the truck. The animal's ability to produce inexhaustible quantities of the stuff was astounding! Could the goat be trying to take over the vehicle by enveloping us in an alien, toxic goo? A picture flashed through my mind of the car slowly dissolving with us inside. Fortunately, the heavy rain combined with the windshield wipers set at warp speed beat back the Green Peril.

The trip ended up taking twelve hours instead of ten because of all the extra stops we made for the goat. Once in Libreville, we made our first stop at Pastor Luc's son's house and unloaded the goat and 400 pounds of wet, green-stained manioc. Now released, the goat wobbled over to a nearby tree, shook itself vigorously and bleated once or twice. Before I got back into the truck, I glanced over at it one more time. I'm sure it had a smirk on its face—unless, of course, I imagined it.

Despite its resilience, the goat played a key role in Ilobo's family celebration several days later, though not exactly as the guest of honor.

I've often thought about that goat and how I made it suffer. I got it to Libreville alive, and it ended up getting eaten, but somehow I had the feeling it had bested me.

Maybe that's because the only real victories are moral ones.

Chapter
Seventeen

PREACHING WET

When Pastor Luc Mambela invited me to accompany him to the four villages of Nzingui, Mbelenaletembet, Yissinga and Nzoundou the next Sunday to preach, I accepted with pleasure. That year, Pastor Luc had been given the huge responsibility of pastoring the large Bongolo church and five of its daughter churches while also serving as the hospital administrator. I wanted to help him in any way I could.

All four villages are situated on a dirt road that a logging company built years ago. It snakes through dense rain forest and passes over countless streams and small rivers that run toward the north-flowing Ngounié River. Since the road was relatively well-maintained, we did not anticipate that getting to the villages on the upcoming Sunday would present a problem.

I was glad for the opportunity to teach the Word of God in villages where many lived who had been treated at our hospital. The people knew who I was, and I had hopefully won some measure of their respect. As I prepared my sermon, I pictured myself standing in front of them, simply but neatly dressed, talking to an attentive and friendly crowd about God's Word.

That Saturday evening, a huge storm front moved in, dumping six inches of rain in four hours. After the heaviest part of the storm passed, it continued to drizzle until morning.

Despite the rain, I was not concerned. After all, the Lord was with us, we were doing His work, and we had a magnificent Nissan Patrol with a powerful winch. *Perhaps,* I thought as I got out of bed and looked at the dripping trees, *perhaps the rain would make the people want to go to church instead of going to work in their gardens.*

We left Bongolo at about 6:30 a.m. in a heavy mist. The Patrol slid around some on the muddy roads, but the mud tires and churning wheels conquered every hill and mud hole. We were about ten kilometers from the first village when we pulled up to a forty-foot-long unfinished log bridge.

A government road maintenance crew had rebuilt the bridge the week before using four massive fifty-foot-long hardwood logs. The bridge spanned a deep ravine carved out by a fast-flowing stream. The center of the log bridge was at least twenty feet above the water.

The road crew had begun to nail eight-inch-thick hardwood beams crossways on the four logs at six-inch intervals, but ten feet from our end of the bridge, they had run out of beams! Someone had shoveled a load of dirt on the exposed logs to make it passable, but the rain had turned the dirt to liquid mud. To get up onto the crossbeams, I would have to drive the first ten feet on top of the mud and bare logs.

Pastor Luc volunteered to walk out onto the bridge to direct me. I put the truck in low four-wheel drive and started out, watching his hands. My front wheels were apparently centered on logs because he held his hands straight up and down and motioned me forward. I surged forward, but when my front tires reached the first six-inch thick crossbeam the truck stopped. I would need a quick surge of power to climb onto it.

I backed the vehicle up about four feet, then stepped on the accelerator. The front wheels leaped forward, but the back wheels spun and slid sideways off the logs. The front of the car lurched to the left and stopped abruptly as I slammed on the brakes. Now, my front wheels were up on the crossbeams but were so close to the edge that the front-end bumper hung out over space.

I got out and looked under the car to see what had happened. Both rear wheels were mired in soft mud down between the logs, and the axle rested solidly on one of the logs.

Pastor Luc and I walked around the truck pondering what to do. It looked to me like I might be able to use the winch on the front bumper to pull the front end of the car over to the center of the bridge. If that worked, then maybe the winch could drag the truck out of the hole and up onto the crossbeams.

Pastor Luc thought my idea might work, so I unwound fifty feet of cable from the winch and attached it to the far end of the bridge. When we were ready, I flipped the switch to turn on the winch. Nothing happened. I couldn't believe it! The winch had never failed to work! I tried toggling the switch, shaking it and finally banging the winch housing, but the winch refused to respond. We gave up and went back to look at the rear wheels.

"Someone," I said to Pastor Luc, thinking it would be him, "will have to crawl under there, push the jack under the axle, jack it up until the differential is off the log, and put rocks under the tires so they grab." I looked over at Pastor Luc to see if he had caught my meaning, but he suddenly stood and went off to look for rocks to put under the tires. Where did he think he was going? Didn't he know I was a surgeon? I looked down at my freshly ironed Dockers, my light cotton shirt and matching tie and wondered what I had been thinking when I got dressed that morning.

Muttering to myself about the unfairness of it all, I removed the tie, got on all fours behind the truck and, gripping the heavy jack, gingerly crawled toward the axle. The space was small, so small in fact that the only way I could get anywhere near the axle was to lie flat on my stomach. I wriggled forward on a slippery bed of something. It was probably just rotting plant fibers, but it smelled like something unspeakable.

As I neared the axle, a blob of mud slid between my skin and my belt. *I can't believe this is happening!* I thought, barely suppressing my rage and frustration. As I advanced, more mud slithered under my belt and into my underwear. Pastor Luc showed up with a piece of wood. I took it and dug mud out from between the logs. As I worked, the mud oozed between the buttons of my shirt, down my collar, even into my shirt sleeves. My neck muscles grew tired from holding my head out of the slime, so I decided to rest it on my arms. By the time I finally got the jack into position, I had mud in my mustache, my eyebrows, my ears, even my nose.

After what seemed like an eternity, I got the jack settled firmly on rock jammed between the logs under the axle. All I needed was the jack handle. I crawled back out from under the car and stood up. As I did so, the mud that had wormed its way into my pants and under my shirt now followed the law of gravity. It did not help at all to see Pastor Luc staring at me, doing his best not to laugh. I knelt again in the mud, attached the handle to the jack and began to crank. A minute later, the axle lifted off the log.

It took us another hour to jam enough rocks and pieces of wood under the wheels to give them traction. The hard work made me perspire heavily and turned the mud inside my clothing to liquid. I had not had that sensation since about the age of two.

When all was ready, Pastor Luc again volunteered to direct me. To my considerable satisfaction, he had not escaped the mud either. Before we tried to drive the truck up onto the beams again, he suggested that we ask God to help us and to keep the car from sliding off the edge of the bridge. I was glad to let him pray.

When he was finished, I covered the front seat with rags, climbed in and turned the front wheels away from the edge. I knew that if the front wheels slipped, the rear wheels would push the car over the side.

"Is this really what You had in mind for us today, Father?" I prayed irritably. "Please help us to get safely over this bridge and out of this mud!" My heart was swirling with a mixture of frustration and fear as I stepped on the accelerator and lunged the truck forward. The front wheels grabbed the wooden beams, the rear wheels spun briefly, and as Pastor Luc shouted and cheered the car surged up onto the middle of the bridge. I bowed my head in relief and gratitude.

On the other side of the bridge I climbed out and walked down to the stream to try to clean up. I was so filthy that I simply immersed myself in the stream fully clothed. The worst of the mud washed away, but despite vigorous scrubbing my pants and shirt remained an uneven, splotchy brown. Pastor Luc waded in and rinsed off his shoes and pant legs. We had no towels, so we climbed back into the truck dripping wet.

A crowd of about fifty men, women, children, dogs, goats and curious chickens had gathered at the mud-brick church and were waiting patiently for us when we arrived. If they found our appearance unusual, they gave no sign of it, singing, clapping in unison and welcoming us with wide smiles. We slogged to the front of the church, leaving large muddy footprints on the cement floor.

Fifteen minutes later, it was my turn to preach. In my stained, dripping clothes I told them that I had come to tell them about my love for Jesus, that it was Jesus who had saved me from my own sin and failure, and who loved me enough to die for me. Pastor Luc stood beside me in an almost-matching outfit and translated my message into the people's own language.

That day, we preached four times in four different villages. Each time I tried my best to explain why everyone should love Jesus and serve Him. Had anyone else died for them? Had anyone else cared that so many of their children died too soon? Did anyone else care that they needed medical care and vaccinations? Jesus did, and He had sent us to help them. He had also died for their sins, not just mine. Though I acted as though I didn't care about my appearance, I had never felt so humiliated in my life.

Some   time later, I was again invited to preach at those same four villages. Confident that lightning wouldn't strike twice, I agreed to go. I invited a cardiologist named Ron Johannsen, who was visiting the hospital, to go along. Ron had come several times before to help out at the hospital, and over the years we had become close friends.

The evening before we were to leave, a storm front moved into the area and dumped six inches of rain in four hours. It drizzled the rest of the night. I should have wondered about the weather, but somehow it didn't register.

Since Ron was the only person riding with me, I decided to take a small, four-wheel drive Suzuki Samurai instead of the big Nissan Patrol. We left Bongolo at 7 a.m. and were not surprised to find the road muddy and slippery. The little car spun and fishtailed repeatedly but never stopped moving forward. Several times we powered through deep, water- filled mudholes in four-wheel drive. Then we came to a ten-foot wide, flood-swollen stream.

I had easily forded the same stream earlier in the week after a rainstorm, so I was confident that it would not be a major problem. Slipping into four-wheel drive, I eased the Suzuki into the water. The front bumper and headlights went underwater, and then the car leveled off. Suddenly, the car slid left into a hole. We lurched, leaned thirty degrees to the side, and nearly stalled as water flowed up over part of the hood. I tried to back out of the hole, but the wheels just spun. Water poured through the leaky door seals and rose to our laps. Ron grabbed his camera, and I grabbed my Bible and songbooks to keep them dry. The car was firmly stuck in four feet of water! We climbed out the door that was still above water and waded to shore.

As the two of us stood dripping on the bank, I tried to figure out what to do next. I always carried a tow strap and a hand winch in the Suzuki, so I waded back in and eventually fished the two items out of the muddy water in the back of the car. Although we were surrounded by trees, the strap and hand winch wouldn't reach even the nearest one. The only possibility was a small clump of bamboo. A mature bamboo stalk is as strong as cable and almost impossible to pull out by the roots, so I pulled the nearest stalk to the ground and tied the tow strap to the end of it. Ron waded in and hooked the winch to a towing hook under the front bumper. The two of us took turns on the winch until the car started inching out of the hole. Then it stopped moving.

Ron suggested that I try to drive the Suzuki out while he maintained pressure with the winch, so I waded back in and settled into the driver's seat. Since the water came up above my waist, I had to feel for the clutch and accelerator with my feet. Fortunately, the ignition key was just above the water line.

The car started on the third try, its exhaust bubbling up behind like an outboard motor. I revved it, let out the clutch, and the little car surged up onto dry land. Ron was doing some kind of victory dance and nearly got run over.

An hour later, we arrived at the first scheduled service and squeegied down the aisle to the front of the church. We were no longer dripping, but we both had muddy water lines on our shirts at the mid-chest level.

I preached four times that day in wet clothes, and perhaps because it had happened before or because Ron was there to enjoy it with me, I didn't mind at all. I wasn't quite sure what had changed, but something had.

I'm not sure if I convinced anyone to give his or her life to Jesus during those two preaching trips, although I may have. I'm not even sure now that preaching to those people was what God was trying to do that day. One night a few months later when I couldn't sleep, it dawned on me that God might really be more interested in keeping me humble than in hearing me preach great sermons.

Chapter
Eighteen

THE UNLIKELY
MINISTER
(GRACE, PART V)

One month after our visit to Yissinga to confront Grace's grandmother, the director of social services in Lebamba came to the hospital to talk to Terry and me about Grace. We were surprised at his sudden interest.

After Cornelia's death we had asked him if there was any way he could help, but he had only shrugged his shoulders and told us to let Grace's family handle the problem. Now he explained that he had changed his mind and had recently looked into her situation.

He had gone to Yissinga to see how she was doing and had concluded that she was being inadequately cared for and very much at risk. Then he made a trip to Libreville to present her case to his superiors. His superiors urged him to intervene and to place Grace with either Veronica and her husband in Franceville or bring her to Libreville to be put up for adoption.

During this time, the mayor who had told us his hands were tied had been abruptly and inexplicably replaced. The director of social services to the new mayor told him the whole convoluted story, but the new mayor did not want to get involved. In his view, it was purely a matter for social services to handle.

Sensing that the social services director wanted to help but that he was feeling vulnerable, I asked him if Terry and I could pray for him. He was surprised, but agreed. We sat in a small circle, bowed our heads and prayed that God would bless this man who according to Scripture was one of God's special ministers. We asked God to protect him from any sorcery Grace's family might try to use against him, to give him unusual courage and boldness to do what was right and best for Grace and to give him wisdom. When we opened our eyes, he thanked us with a look of amazement. We had no idea what an impact that prayer would have on him.

Two or three weeks later, the director asked Pastor Luc, Terry and I to attend a meeting in his office with the mayor. It was a busy weekday morning, but since it seemed important, we canceled our appointments at the hospital and drove to his office in Lebamba.

He was obviously nervous as he seated us on rickety metal chairs. His two secretaries sat at empty desks with nothing to do, trying hard to ignore us. The mayor, he explained with obvious embarrassment, had declined to meet with us. Nevertheless, he wanted to report what he was trying to do. He had gone to Yissinga and on his own authority had ordered Grace's grandmother to come to his office with Grace to meet with us. He had given her money for the trip, and he fully expected her to come. He had also sent an official message to his counterpart in Franceville ordering Veronica to come to Lebamba to explain her failure to take Grace with her to Franceville.

We waited for two hours. It soon became obvious that Grace's grandmother was not going to show. We were not surprised, but we managed to hide our disappointment. We prayed with him again before leaving.

There was no more news about Grace for another month. Then, in April of 1998, the director came to the hospital again and asked to see us. Veronica had come to Yissinga and had reportedly taken Grace back to Franceville without stopping in Lebamba to talk to him. He wondered if we would be willing to contact our missionaries in Franceville to check on her. We agreed to send them an e-mail and to ask them to be on the lookout for Veronica and Grace.

In May, we heard from Ray and Maureen Holcomb, our missionaries in Franceville. A woman holding a little girl had come up to them after church and introduced herself as Veronica. She had then presented to them the little girl named Grace. The Holcombs invited Veronica and Grace to their house for dinner and spent a pleasant afternoon with them. Grace appeared to be well cared for and happy. Her new mother explained that she, Grace and the rest of her family regularly attended one of the Alliance churches in Franceville.

In the year since then, Grace has developed into an affectionate and happy child and remains part of a loving Christian family. If she remembers any of the events of the terrible first two years of her life, she does not show it. Although she has never returned to either Yissinga or Bongolo, she will always remain our hospital's child.

Jesus said, "See that you do not look down on one of these little ones. For I tell you that their angels in heaven always see the face of my Father in heaven" (Matthew 18:10). Like a mother eagle, God swooped down and lifted little Grace out of a life of squalor and hopelessness and gave her instead a life filled with love.

Chapter
Nineteen

THE POLICE STOP

In spite of the lack of high-tech equipment or even standard lab tests, my medical practice in Africa has been delightful compared to the practice of medicine in America today. I don't have to worry about malpractice insurance because nobody wants to sue the only board-certified surgeon within 200 miles. Managed care is not only incomprehensible in most of the developing world, it's virtually unknown. In my practice, the doctor and patient and his family make all the decisions about health care, and medical services are paid for in either cash, goats or assigned work.

This seemingly idyllic and stress-free arrangement between health care providers and patients might at times tempt physicians and nurses in North America to consider giving up their practices to serve as missionaries in Africa. Before anyone does that, however, he or she should probably know about police stops.

The police in much of Africa have few cars. Instead, they control the roads with check points, harassing drivers and wielding near-total power. They have little need for written laws since they seem to be authorized to make up laws on the spot. This is tolerated by governments because the police also occasionally nab criminals on the run, identify illegal immigrants, make sure that tourists don't take the right to photograph their country for granted and collect from travelers enough francs to keep them from being paid less than army privates.

On average, the trip between Libreville and Bongolo, a distance of 350 miles, is punctuated by between five and ten police stops. This pattern holds true for travel on most major routes throughout Central and West Africa.

I was returning from a month of training in eye surgery in Ebolowa, Cameroon a few years ago and decided to take the most direct route back to Gabon by traveling in public transportation. I took a taxi to the town's central marketplace and climbed out near a collection of beat-up vans, compact pickup trucks and ancient SUVs that all qualified as "taxibuses." Since there were no buses heading to the Gabonese border, I climbed into an old Nissan taxibus.

The van was designed to hold eight people, but the owner had added a seat in the front by inserting a cushioned chair between the bucket seats. The front seats were already filled, so I took one of the spots in the second row. Within thirty minutes the bus was crammed with five people in the back seat, four in my row and three in the front, including the driver. All our bags were tied onto the roof.

We got only as far as the edge of town before encountering the first police stop. I presented my passport to a policeman and was told to get out and sit in one of five chairs lined up under a tree by the road. Three or four others from the bus joined me. A few minutes later, a policeman came along with a small pad of forms. When I asked him why I was being detained, he explained that I could not leave town without paying for a departure permit. Since it cost only about $5, it seemed pointless to argue. Once I had my permit, I was allowed back into the van with the others.

Ten minutes down the road, three women waved the van to a stop and asked to get on. To my surprise, the driver took their money and indicated that they were to sit in "my" row which already held four men. Since there was no possibility of squeezing another person onto the seat, the ladies simply sat on our laps. Fortunately, the woman who sat on my lap didn't weigh too much. I learned somewhat belatedly that if you don't want the driver to put a passenger on your lap, you should pay for two seats!

After an hour of driving, we approached a town, and the driver informed me that I would have to change to another taxibus to get to the border. Instead of driving to the marketplace where the taxibuses loaded and unloaded their passengers, he drove a mile out of the way to the police station and ordered me off. When I asked him why, he explained that all tourists and foreigners were required to report to the police.

I carried my bags into the police station and stood in a dingy hallway just inside the door, wondering what to do next. Eventually, a young uniformed policeman came out of a doorway. He immediately asked to see my passport. After looking at every page several times, he asked why I had not purchased a permit to travel through that particular province. I was speechless with surprise, but managed to explain that I had gotten a visa to his country that permitted me to travel anywhere in the country. I then produced the permit I had purchased earlier.

With a serious look on his face, he shook his head.

"I'm afraid you are mistaken, Monsieur. You will not be allowed to proceed to the next town until you have purchased your permit. They are not expensive—only $20. The permit you purchased in Ebolowa only allows you to leave Ebolowa, not travel outside of Ebolowa."

I nearly started laughing. Then I got mad.

"I'm not paying for any permit to travel in this province. I have a legal visa in my passport that authorizes me to travel from town to town and province to province without any permit, so I'm not paying anything."

There was a bench in the hallway, so I dragged my suitcase over to it and sat down. The gendarme frowned briefly, then shrugged and walked off with my passport. I sat in the hallway for an hour while people walked in and out and ignored me.

I was just beginning to wonder if I hadn't made a tactical blunder when the young gendarme returned—with my passport.

"Come with me," he said. "I've explained your situation to the chief of police. He wants to see what you look like." Then he added, "Do you smoke?" I shook my head, and so did he.

This sounded alarming, and I wondered what if anything I could do to appear completely innocuous. Should I tell them I'm a doctor? A surgeon? Or would that just result in demands for more money? I prayed a silent prayer to the Lord for wisdom and calm as I followed the man down the hall.

The gendarme opened the door and ushered me into a small room full of smoke and talk. A large man sat behind a desk in the center of the room, smoke curling upward from the cigarette between his lips. Four African men stood in front of him, their passports on his desk next to mine. All had been talking and gesturing when we entered, but when I walked in, everyone stopped talking.

The young gendarme started talking to the chief of police in another language. The chief scowled at me. For at least thirty seconds he scowled, as though trying to communicate the frailty of my position by mental telepathy. Then, without a word, he picked up my passport and handed it to me. I grabbed it, but for another five seconds he held onto it as if to underline the power he had over me. Then he let it go, and the young gendarme hustled me out of the room.

"You may go now," he said. "You've been granted an exemption." With that, he turned on his heels and walked down the hall.

It took me an hour to walk the mile to the marketplace, dragging my heavy suitcase and shoulder bag down the dusty road. I soon found another ride, this time sharing a bucket seat in the front of a Toyota Roadrunner with a fourteen-year-old boy. I made it across the border into Gabon before nightfall without further incident.

On another occasion Becki and I were driving from Bongolo to Libreville with our fourteen-year-old son, Jeremy. He was asleep in the backseat when we came around a corner and saw the familiar signs of a police stop—three battered drums standing in the road. Two policemen were sitting on chairs in the shade of a tree next to the road. When we stopped, one of them stood and came over to the car.

I had my driver's license, vehicle papers and visa in hand. He looked over them carefully to see if they were all in order. When he finished, he handed them back to me. His eyes flickered to the seat behind me where Jeremy slept.

"Wake him up!" he ordered gruffly. Surprised, I explained that Jeremy was my son and was only a boy.

"I said wake him up! Everyone must be awake and sitting up at a police stop!" I turned and woke Jeremy. He sat up and looked at the glaring policeman in complete bewilderment. Apparently satisfied, the policeman waved us through.

Another time, when I traveled to Cameroon, the immigration officer at the Douala airport studied my passport for more than a minute.

"This visa is not valid," the officer said, looking at me suspiciously. I had gotten it only two days earlier at the Cameroonese embassy in Libreville, so I knew it was valid. I asked him what was wrong with it.

"It's dated last year," he answered. Sure enough, the embassy official had written the wrong year on my visa! I suddenly remembered that I still had the receipt in my wallet. I had never kept a receipt for a visa before, but for some reason I had tucked this one away. I pulled it out and showed the officer that it was properly dated. He scowled at the receipt for a minute, then told me to follow him. We walked for five minutes through dimly lit hallways, our footsteps echoing on the bare cement floors until we came to a small waiting room outside the central police office. The officer pointed me to a rickety metal chair next to about twenty African men who for some reason were sitting quietly on the floor. As I sat down, my eye caught a glimmer of steel on their wrists. They were all chained together. A few minutes later the officer came out and stood next to me.

Overcome with curiosity, I asked him, "Why are these men here?" He looked at them with disdain.

"They're here because they had counterfeit visas when they got off the plane!" My heart sank to my toes.

Ten minutes later the customs officer and I were called into the office where the chief of police sat. He compared the visa in my passport with the receipt I had produced. After a moment he smiled and said, "This is not your fault. You may go." He must have seen the relief on my face because he laughed and waved me out the door. As I walked past the men on the floor and down the hall to freedom, I wondered what would have happened had I not kept my receipt.

Several years later, I drove to Libreville to buy a set of wicker living room furniture for an apartment we had just built to house our African surgery residents. The set included four armchairs, a sofa and a matching coffee table. Because without the cushions the entire set didn't weigh more than 100 pounds, I tied all of it up on the roof rack with about fifty feet of rope. When I finished, the effect of all that furniture looming six feet above the top of my car was somewhat surreal.

At 7 a.m. the next morning I pulled out of Libreville and headed down to Bongolo. I had gone about eighty miles and was near the end of the paved road when I came to the first police stop. Both gendarmes stood to their feet as I came into view. A bad sign! The older one blew his whistle vigorously. I knew I was in trouble although I wasn't sure what law I had broken. The two men were staring at the tangle of furniture and rope when I walked around the back of the truck. The man with the whistle regarded me soberly and without a trace of humor said, "Vehicle abuse."

In spite of my effort to show no reaction, my eyebrows shot up in surprise. I had never heard of vehicle abuse. My eyebrows must have given me away because he motioned for me to follow him back to his table and chair. He sat down and pulled out his receipt book.

"You can't load your vehicle with that much stuff," he explained.

"But it's not heavy," I protested. "You know how wicker furniture is. It doesn't even weigh 100 pounds."

"It's too high," he replied.

"It's lower than the rail overpass and doesn't stick up as high as the logging trucks," I insisted. "It doesn't endanger or impede other vehicles. My roof rack is designed to carry 500 pounds."

He shook his head and gave me a look that indicated he was growing weary of the discussion.

"It's vehicle abuse," he said firmly. It seemed best to concede, so I asked him how much the fine was for vehicle abuse.

"Three thousand francs (about \$5)," he said, looking as though he had made a huge concession to me. I handed him the money, he filled out a small receipt, signed it and gave it to me. I was walking back to the truck when I thought of something.

"What's going to happen at the next police stop?" I asked. "Am I going to have to pay at every stop?" The gendarme shook his head.

"That's why I gave you a receipt. If you're stopped again, just show the gendarme the receipt, and he'll let you go on without paying again." Reassured, I waved and drove through the opening his partner made between the barrels.

Fifteen minutes later I sailed around a corner and screeched to a halt at another police stop. Several cars and trucks were parked on the opposite side of the road in the oncoming lane, and another car was parked in front of me. A young man rolled one of the barrels out of the way as I approached. Thinking I was getting the green light to proceed, I slowly drove through the opening. That idea evaporated with the shrilling of a police whistle to my left. I stopped and looked up a low bank on the left side of the road where a crowd of drivers stood in front of a small shack. A lone gendarme stood behind a table, holding a whistle to his lips and pointing right at me.

The gendarme must have said something funny to the drivers in front of him because as I approached everyone started laughing. A well-dressed man got out of a car behind me and called to the gendarme, "Hey, this ought to be good!" The gendarme laughed and said something unintelligible. By the time I reached the top of the bank it seemed like thirty people were staring at me and either smirking, chuckling or covering their mouths.

If I had smiled back at them I might have been OK, but instead I gritted my teeth and turned red.

"Please help me to stay calm, Lord," I prayed. "This man apparently doesn't know who I am."

The big gendarme kept standing as I approached and scowled at me as I stepped up to his table.

"Monsieur," he said, waving at the car with one hand, "you are not permitted to do that to your car." Several in the crowd snickered. I answered as calmly as I could, knowing I had the receipt from the last police stop in my pocket.

"Monsieur le Gendarme," I responded, "all that furniture weighs less than 100 pounds. It looks like a great deal of weight, but it is very light."

"Did you weigh it?" he asked sarcastically. This produced an explosion of guffaws from the onlookers.

"No, I didn't weigh it, but you know how light wicker furniture is. My car rack is designed to carry 500 pounds, and I'm sure that furniture weighs far less than that."

"But you didn't weigh it, did you?"

"No," I answered reluctantly.

"Well, there you are. You'll pay me a fine."

Pulling the receipt out of my pocket, I said to him, "I already got stopped fifteen minutes ago and paid a fine. Here's my receipt."

He looked at me with mock astonishment, then burst out laughing.

"Was I there? Did you see me?" He turned to the crowd for effect, and even the kids giggled. I was seething inside, but still managed to stay calm.

"I should not have to pay this fine twice."

"Oh, we have a smart one here," he said sarcastically. Then placing both hands palm down on the table in front of him he locked eyes with me and said, "If you think you're going to continue down this road without paying me a fine, you underestimate me. This is my country not yours. You can either pay me or turn your car around and go back to Libreville."

I should have remained quiet or shrugged or done something—anything but what I did. I was angry and humiliated, and I resented the fact that despite almost 100 trips up and down that road this man was treating me like garbage. Everybody along that road knew about our hospital, everybody knew who I was and what my truck looked like. There was even a sign on the door clearly identifying me as an Alliance missionary. I had operated on so many policemen's relatives it was impossible that this man did not know who he was talking to.

Holding my wrists together in front of me I said to him, "Why don't you just arrest me and take me to the Lambaréné jail? Because I'm not going to pay that fine again."

For about three seconds you could have heard a leaf drop to the ground. Nobody seemed to be breathing except me. Then the gendarme sort of swelled, as if he had inhaled too much air. His eyes bulged slightly, and he stood directly in front of me.

"White man," he said loudly, "you can sit here all night if you want, but you're not going past this police stop until you pay me." He turned and stalked out to the other cars on the road.

Twenty minutes later my pride had crawled off somewhere and was near death. When the policeman had finished making the other drivers pay their fines for whatever sins they had committed, I too paid and walked back to my truck. To my surprise, my fatally wounded pride miraculously revived and bounded back into the truck with me as I drove away.

If God didn't humiliate surgeons from time to time, could anyone stand them?

Chapter
Twenty

THE GIRL WHO
COULDN'T BREATHE

When Deb Walker, our pediatrician, called me on the CB radio at 2 a.m. I was so groggy that it took me about three minutes to understand what she was talking about. All I heard was something about a girl who couldn't breathe and had been taken into the operating room.

It was dark and raining when I unlocked the garage doors and swung them open. But I hardly noticed. *Why in the world,* I thought grumpily, *did I need to go down for a case of asthma?*

I drove down the hill, pulled to a stop in front of the surgery building and pushed through the group of anxious family members clustered around the front door trying to see what was going on inside.

The girl on the operating table was about eighteen years old. In spite of the oxygen mask on her face and her wide desperate eyes, I could tell that she was beautiful. Her chest was heaving as she gasped and coughed up pink, frothy fluid into an emesis basin one of our nurses held next to her mouth. Deb listened to the girl's chest with her stethoscope while one nursing student took the girl's blood pressure and another placed a clip from the oxygen monitor on one of the girl's fingertips. The nurses in the ER had already inserted an IV in one arm.

"The nurses called me to the ER an hour ago when the family brought this girl in," Deb explained. "They thought she was having an asthma attack. But this is much more than an asthma attack. Her lungs are full of fluid, like someone in congestive heart failure."

It didn't make sense that a perfectly healthy eighteen-year-old would suddenly develop congestive heart failure. The name written on the chart was Madeleine. I asked Deb if either Madeleine or her family had given any information about how the illness had started.

"She told us that she started having trouble breathing a couple of hours ago, all of a sudden. She swears that she drank nothing unusual, smoked nothing, did nothing to herself and has never had a problem like this before." The girl's worsening condition made less and less sense. "She's also about six weeks pregnant," Deb added. A lightbulb turned on in my head.

"Did you find any traditional medicines in her vagina?" I asked. Young women in Gabon frequently kill their unborn babies by placing a concoction of poisonous leaves and bark in their vaginas. The "remedy" usually works, but it can also poison the mother.

"I already thought of that," Deb answered. "The answer is 'no.' "

Just about then the oxygen monitor began to chirp. I glanced at it and saw that Madeleine's oxygen level was below eighty-five percent, an ominous sign for someone already on 100 percent oxygen with a normal blood pressure. As I repeated the physical examination I noted that she was spitting up more and more frothy, pink fluid. Her lungs were filling up so rapidly that she was literally drowning. *Could this be some kind of hemorrhagic fever like ebola fever?* I wondered to myself. If so, we were all going to come down with it in another day or two.

I finally intubated Madeleine by placing a plastic tube into her trachea. This made it possible to suction out her lungs. I did that every two to three minutes for a while, then reconnected her to the anesthesia machine to give her oxygen. The procedure finally increased her oxygen level to ninety percent, and we began to feel more optimistic. But we still didn't know what was causing the girl's bizarre symptoms.

Madeleine couldn't talk with a tube in her throat, but I needed to find out if she wanted to change her story. Putting my mouth next to her ear, I asked her if in the last twenty-four hours she had swallowed poison or eaten food that she had not prepared herself.

She shook her head.

Then I asked her if she had put poison in her vagina to kill her baby. Again, she shook her head.

About that time our chaplain, Boukila Simon, arrived. After explaining to him what was happening, we asked him to pray for the girl. He knelt next to her ear and after introducing himself, prayed that God would intervene to save her life and would give us wisdom on how best to treat her. A moment later her oxygen level dropped below eighty-five percent. Five minutes later, despite all our efforts, it dropped below eighty percent.

I shook my head and told Boukila Simon that we thought the girl was hiding something from us. The clinical picture didn't make any sense. If she would just tell us what happened, we might be able to think of other ways to help her. He knelt next to her and once again spoke quietly into her ear, explaining that unless God intervened, we didn't know if we could save her. Was there anything she could tell us that might help. She was conscious, and she heard, but this time she did not shake her head.

"Did you put poison in your vagina to kill your baby?" he asked.

Her oxygen level dropped below seventy-five percent. For a moment, I thought she had lost consciousness and wasn't hearing him. Then she nodded her head. Her oxygen level dropped to seventy percent, sixty-five percent, then sixty percent. The girl was no longer conscious. At any moment she would arrest, and it would be over. Desperate, I asked everyone in the operating room to be quiet while I prayed one more time.

"Father," I cried out, my voice shaking with emotion, "please give this girl another chance. She doesn't know You, and if she dies now, it will be too late. We've done all we know to do, and it's not enough. Please touch her and reverse the effect of the poisons she has put in her body. Please give her another chance! Amen."

The oxygen monitor is designed to beep at different pitches, depending on the oxygen level being recorded. When the oxygen level is high, the tone of the beep is higher, and when it is low, the tone is lower. While I was praying for her, the pitch of the beep remained low and moved lower. But less than ten seconds after I said "amen," the pitch moved up. We turned and looked at the monitor. The oxygen level was inexplicably moving up.

A minute later it climbed above seventy percent. Five minutes later it reached seventy-five percent, and fifteen minutes later it had risen to eighty-five percent—even though we weren't doing anything different than we had done for the previous thirty minutes. An hour later, after the girl's oxygen level reached ninety-four percent, we extubated her and moved her to a hospital bed, giving her oxygen by mask. God had heard our prayer and had saved her life.

I wish I could report that she gave her heart to Christ after she heard what God had done for her, but she didn't. She left the hospital the next day and returned home. I assume that her baby died and passed out of her body. What I do know is that God is still giving her another chance. I still pray that someday she will give her heart to the Savior.

God still heals people today using supernatural, extra-medical power. Some who doubt that God still works in supernatural ways in our bodies in response to prayer might say that Madeleine recovered because the medical measures we employed allowed her to live just long enough for her body's natural defenses to win out over the poison she used. Others would not call this a true miracle because doctors and nurses and medicines were involved.

There is a story in the Bible found in Isaiah 38:1-5 that tells about a Jewish king named Hezekiah. Hezekiah was a good and godly king, but one day he fell seriously ill. Isaiah the prophet tells the story himself:

> "This is what the LORD says: Put your house in order, because you are going to die; you will not recover."
>
> Hezekiah turned his face to the wall and prayed to the LORD, "Remember, O LORD, how I have walked before you faithfully and with whole-hearted devotion and have done what is good in your eyes." And Hezekiah wept bitterly.
>
> Then the word of the LORD came to Isaiah: "Go and tell Hezekiah, 'This is what the LORD, the God of your father David, says: I have heard your

prayer and seen your tears: I will add fifteen years
to your life.' "

Then Isaiah said to him, "Prepare a poultice of figs and apply it to the boil, and he will recover" (38:21). This was apparently done, and Hezekiah recovered.

So what healed Hezekiah? God's power or figs? Only someone who does not believe that God can and does intervene supernaturally in His creation would say it was the figs. The figs played a part in Hezekiah's healing, but knowing what I do about what poultices can do, I doubt they played the major part. God used *both* natural and supernatural means to heal the good king Hezekiah.

He continues to do so to this day. Read on.

Chapter
Twenty-One

TWO HANDS

I n early 2000, a four-year-old boy came to our hospital with an intestinal obstruction. He was near death from vomiting and dehydration when he came, but with antibiotics and intravenous fluids we were able to reverse his state of shock and sepsis. I took him to the operating room fully expecting to find him full of worms. Instead, I found his abdomen full of cancer.

The boy's intestinal obstruction was caused by masses of tumors throughout his small intestine. The tumors had migrated to his liver and spleen, and there were tumor implants throughout his abdominal cavity. With a sinking heart, I removed the portion of his intestine that was completely obstructed and sewed it back together. This would enable him to live and eventually to resume eating, but would not control the extensive cancer in his abdomen. A biopsy of the tumor eventually revealed it to be a highly invasive cancer not very sensitive to chemotherapy or radiation.

When we finished the operation I found the boy's mother waiting anxiously outside the operating room. She was a single mother, and the boy was her only child. Her face was streaked with tears. As gently as I could, I explained to her what I had found and told her that only God could heal her boy. Her eyes grew round with horror, and she broke into loud cries. Then she fell to the ground at my feet, sobbing, beating her head against the cement floor, heartbroken. Other patients came over and tried to comfort her, some of them crying with her, but she was so overcome I could say little more and had to leave her with others.

The next day when she was calmer and sitting next to her sleeping child, our chaplain came by to see her. As they talked, she suddenly stopped and said, "Pastor, the doctor told me yesterday that only God could heal my child. What did he mean by that?"

Over the next thirty minutes the chaplain told her about Jesus and how He had healed people while He was on earth because He was God visiting earth as a man. The pastor told her the whole story of Jesus and asked her if she wanted to invite Him into her life.

"Yes," she said. After they prayed, the chaplain asked her if she believed that Jesus could heal her son.

"The doctor thinks He can!" she replied.

"Do you?" he asked. After a moment, she said, "Yes."

"Then let's pray and ask Him," the chaplain said. Placing a gentle hand on the sleeping boy, he did.

A week later we took the stitches out of the boy's abdominal incision. He was eating well, sitting up and walking around, but not demonstrably healed of his cancer. I could still feel a mass in his liver along with some others. Because the family lived some distance away, I gave the mother an appointment to come back in a month.

"Aren't you going to give me any medicine for my son?" she asked, disappointment evident in her eyes. I told her no, because he wasn't experiencing any pain and nothing I could give him would do much for him. Then I added something I later regretted.

"In America or France we could give your son some strong medicines to prolong his life; but they would not be able to cure him of the cancer."

The boy's mother sat up straighter.

"Could you give me a prescription so I could try to get them in Libreville?" she asked with renewed hope.

I tried to discourage her, telling her how expensive the chemotherapy drugs would be, that they would be hard to find and that she would have to come back to the hospital with the medicines and the boy because the treatment was complicated. But she would not be deterred. In the end I wrote the prescription.

Four weeks later mother and son missed their appointment. I thought he had probably succumbed to the cancer and died. But two weeks after that, the mother returned. I was walking from the OR to my office when she approached me.

"I brought the medicines," she said. I recognized her immediately, but where was the boy? Puzzled, I took the bag and looked inside. Every medicine I had prescribed was there. It must have cost her over $500.

"Do you want to sell these?" I asked.

She looked confused. "No, they're for my son!" Just then a boy who looked at least six years old ran up to her.

"Where is he?" I asked, wondering who the boy was.

She looked even more confused. "He's right here!" It was my turn to look confused. The boy was at least an inch taller and ten pounds heavier than when I had last seen him. I pulled up his shirt, and there was the scar of my operation running across his abdomen. I motioned for them to follow me into the office.

The boy hopped up onto the examining table and grinned at me. He was ticklish, and I had to calm him down so I could feel for the tumor. When he finally stopped giggling, I felt for his liver. It was smooth and not the least bit enlarged. His spleen was too small to find. There were no lumps or bumps at all in his abdomen where there once had been massive tumors. I examined him for at least five minutes before I gave up.

Turning to the mother, I said simply, "God has healed your son."

A huge smile spread across her face.

"Will he still need the medicine?" In one of the happiest moments of my medical career, I told her no and bought her medicines. We could always use them for someone else.

What healed the boy? Was it my surgery, or was it God? It was both, of course. If I had not operated on the boy the day he first came, he would have died. And if God had not healed him from the cancer, he would have died.

God is the one who designed and made the world and everything that is in it, down to the smallest detail. He created our immune systems and our bodies, and when we are ill, our bodies work to heal themselves, using natural, not supernatural means. God also made all of the medicines that will ever be discovered—knowing which ones would be helpful and which ones would be deadly long before any human figured it out by trial and error. He also created the synthetic medicines that have been and will be discovered, because He created the laws that determine the way atoms and molecules act and interact with each other. Colossians 1:17 says, that "in him all things hold together." Hebrews 1:3 says that He is "sustaining all things by his powerful word."

Not only has God created and placed in our world products that can help our bodies, but God has also given us wonderful gifts of medical knowledge. It is He who reveals to men the wonders of the human body, how the immune system functions to bring healing, how bacteria and viruses destroy and how they can be destroyed or controlled. The scientific method was His idea long before any scientist described it.

There are, therefore, two streams through which God can bring healing to a human body, and neither need exclude the other: he can bring healing through the natural, created responses of our bodies to disease, aided by the medicines He placed in His creation and by the knowledge of disease and healing that He continues to give to those who seek it; *and* He can bring healing using extra-medical means, using His spiritual power.

It should not surprise anyone who believes that the Bible is true that this is so, because the Bible teaches from cover to cover that we live in a universe that is both physical and spiritual. There are physical beings in this world and spiritual beings. We ourselves are more than biological machines: we are a combination of the physical and the spiritual. The blend of both in one body is something so wonderful and mysterious that is continues to defy all attempts to understand it.

God also seems to genuinely want us to partner with Him in His work of redemption here on earth. Why should we exclude the work of healing the sick? Although God does not intervene supernaturally to heal every patient we ask Him to heal, I have *never* seen Him heal supernaturally when nobody asked. That is why I pray for all of my patients. God wants physicians to partner with Him in *both* streams of His provision.

As a missionary physician and surgeon it has been my delight to serve as one of God's junior partners. The hand that guides my scalpel is not just my physical hand: if I will let Him, God's mighty hand will guide my scalpel too.

Twenty-Two

THE BOY WITH THE BURULI ULCER

We first met Donald after a church service in Libreville. Becki and I had returned to Gabon the day before to begin another four-year term of service. We decided to attend a church in the capital city that, in the eighteen years we had been in Gabon, had grown from eight people to more than 3,000.

After the service, we were working our way through the crowd to get to where we had parked our truck when a young woman rushed up to us.

"Are you Dr. Thompson?" she asked breathlessly. I did not really want to hold a clinic in the church parking lot that day, but there was no way to deny it, so I confessed.

"Doctor," she said almost desperately, "my little boy has been in the Central Hospital here in Libreville for four months with a strange infection on his chest. The doctors have tried everything, but the infection just keeps getting worse. Unless you can help him, my husband and I are afraid he's going to die!" Tears filled her eyes as she spoke, and I knew I couldn't refuse. I asked her what she wanted us to do.

"If you will wait right here, my husband and I will go get him from the hospital and bring him here." We agreed to wait. About thirty minutes later, a taxi pulled up to the now empty parking lot.

A muscular man we later learned was Donald's father stepped out of the taxi holding a thin, frightened, eight-year old boy in his arms. After the introductions, we took a few moments to explain to the boy that we just wanted to see the infection, not hurt him. Reluctantly, he pulled up his T-shirt and showed us a six-inch square bandage on the right side of his chest. He allowed me to lift the bandage, and I saw a baseball-sized hole with ragged, undetermined edges. I could see his ribs at the base of the wound. I recognized it as a Buruli ulcer.

Buruli ulcers are named after the town in Africa where they were first described. They are caused by a bacteria named *mycobacterium ulcerans*, a cousin to tuberculosis that infects the skin instead of the lungs. Treatment with even the most modern antibiotics does not seem to alter the course of the disease. Untreated, the infection can go on for years and leave severe scarring, deformities or even death. I had seen Buruli ulcers before, but never one this large or deep.

I told Donald's mother and father that I thought we could help him, but it would involve complete excision of all the infected tissue on his chest. After surgery, the wound would be four or five times larger than it was now. They would have to bring him to our hospital 300 miles to the south and would need to stay for several months. Both parents said they understood and agreed to bring him to Bongolo as soon as possible.

Two or three weeks later, Donald and his mother showed up at the hospital and were admitted to the surgery ward. The next day, we took Donald to the operating room. Before we gave him the anesthetic and while his mother stood next to him and held his hand, we prayed that God would help us, give us wisdom and protect and heal Donald. We also prayed that Donald would meet Jesus and invite Him into his heart during his stay. Once he was asleep, his mother left the OR.

The bacteria that causes Buruli ulcers burrows under the skin and fat where there is minimal air. To expose the base of the wound to the air and to topical disinfectants, the surgeon must mercilessly remove all infected tissue. Donald's infection had spread much farther than we expected, and we were forced to remove the skin and fat over his entire chest. The disease had continued on up into the base of his neck, down over his abdomen and into his groin. Two hours later, when we finished, at least a third of the skin on his body was gone, along with about a pint of blood that we had to partially replace with a transfusion. The wound was appalling.

We covered the raw surfaces with dressings soaked in disinfectant and changed the dressings twice a day. Every time the nurses changed his dressings, we could hear Donald screaming, even from the operating room. Even today that memory brings a lump to my throat and tears to my eyes.

We performed a total of thirteen operations on Donald before we managed to control the infection and start covering his chest and abdomen with skin grafts. He nearly died several times, was transfused five or six times and was hospitalized for five months. Only God knows how he endured the pain and survived.

As the skin grafts grew and the size of his wound closed, his pain diminished, his appetite increased and he gained weight. Midway through his hospitalization, he invited Jesus Christ into his heart. All of us rejoiced that Donald would live forever, no matter what happened to his frail body.

I am deeply grateful to God that He enabled us to help Donald survive his terrible infection. I am even happier that he became one of God's children. Donald was one of the reasons God taught me what I know and sent Becki and me to Gabon. For more than twenty years we have devoted our lives to serving the sick and telling them about Jesus Christ. It is what we hope to do until our strength gives out.

A Word from the Author

God has His own solutions to suffering. The first one is the most obvious: Jesus taught His disciples to share what they had with the poor. He taught that those who are called by His name are to help those who suffer and not to ignore them, blame them or exploit them. We believe that is one reason why God has given North Americans such enormous resources—not so that they can live 100 or 1,000 times better than the rest of the world, but so that they can share their wealth of money, time and expertise to lift millions of people out of poverty, sickness and ignorance.

But that is a temporary solution—not God's final solution for suffering. There are not enough resources in the world to solve all the world's problems. If we think that there are, that mankind can eventually overcome the world's lethal flaws, then we have seriously misunderstood what Jesus taught when He came to earth as God in a human body. What the world really needs is a King—a God-King.

By now, history and the Bible should have convinced those who follow Christ that no mere human will ever bring universal peace, harmony and justice to the world, not to mention health and the promise of eternal life.

As of today, there are an estimated 25 million Africans infected with HIV. Most of them will be dead from AIDS within five years. AIDS mostly kills adults, and it is estimated that by 2002 more than 10 million orphans in Africa will be without adults to care for them. Many, if not most, of these children will die of starvation, neglect, violence or disease.

There is only one way that the world's suffering is going to come to an end, and that is for the One who is called in the Bible the "King of kings and Lord of lords" to come and take control of the earth. When He does (and the Bible clearly teaches that He will) all wars, all suffering, all pain and death will come to an end.

The apostle John saw this in a vision and wrote it down in Revelation 19:11-16:

> I saw heaven standing open and there before me
> was a white horse, whose rider is called Faithful and
> True. With justice he judges and makes war. His
> eyes are like blazing fire, and on his head are many
> crowns. He has a name written on him that no one
> knows but he himself. He is dressed in a robe dipped
> in blood, and his name is the Word of God. The ar-
> mies of heaven were following him, riding on white
> horses and dressed in fine linen, white and clean. Out
> of his mouth comes a sharp sword [the Word of
> God] with which to strike down the nations. "He
> will rule them with an iron scepter." . . . On his robe
> and on his thigh he has this name written:
> KING OF KINGS AND LORD OF LORDS.

And in Revelation 21:3-4, John wrote more about what he saw:

> Now the dwelling of God is with men, and he will
> live with them. They will be his people, and God
> himself will be with them and be their God. He
> will wipe every tear from their eyes. There will be

> no more death or mourning or crying or pain, for
> the old order of things has passed away.

Despite constant wars, hatred, racism, unspeakable atrocities and environmental destruction, some people seem to like the world the way it is. It's the best humans can do, they say. It's the price of democracy or of the free market or some other human explanation that favors the few who have wealth and power to the detriment of others. Some even say that 25 million deaths in Africa from AIDS will ease the world's problem of overpopulation. But few who live among the poor, who try to help those who suffer or who suffer privation or injustice themselves care much for this world as it is.

Becki and I have seen enough suffering in our lifetimes to do us for several lifetimes. Both of my parents, Ed and Ruth Thompson, and Becki's father, Archie Mitchell, were murdered during the Vietnam war. Becki's mother, Betty Mitchell, survived imprisonment in North Vietnam. We long for the King of kings to come and put an end to human suffering. And we want Him to do it as soon as possible.

Few Christians today understand that God has placed in their hands one of the keys to the coming of the King of kings and Lord of lords and to the end of human suffering. After His resurrection and before He went to heaven to be with the Father, Jesus said to His disciples:

> All authority in heaven and on earth has been
> given to me. Therefore go and make disciples of all
> nations, baptizing them in the name of the Father
> and of the Son and of the Holy Spirit, and teaching
> them to obey everything I have commanded you.
> And surely I am with you always, to the very end of
> the age. (Matthew 28:18-20)

Most evangelical Christians call this "The Great Commission." And a few are working hard to obey the Great Commission, even to the point of risking their lives. Others, however, don't seem to think that the Great Commission concerns them personally.

After Jesus returned to heaven, His disciple, Matthew, wrote the following in Matthew 24:14: "And this gospel of the kingdom will be preached in the whole world as a testimony to all nations, *and then the end will come*" [italics mine]. In other words, the end of this world as we know it will not come until the gospel of Jesus is preached "to all nations."

I don't know when He'll return, but it won't be before His Church has turned in the assignment He gave her nearly 2,000 years ago.

What is your agenda about?

God is calling this generation of Christians to take up the cross of "whatever it takes" and finish the job of telling the world about Jesus Christ.

Are you among those out there who are willing to give up their lives to bring back the King?